Nelson *Mathematics* 8

Workbook

Series Authors and Senior Consultants

Marian Small • Mary Lou Kestell

Senior Author

David Zimmer

Workbook Author

Christy Hayhoe

NELSON / E D U C A T I O N

NELSON / EDUCATION

Nelson Mathematics 8
Workbook

Series Authors and
Senior Consultants
Marian Small, Mary Lou Kestell

Senior Author
David Zimmer

Workbook Author
Christy Hayhoe

Director of Publishing
Beverley Buxton

Publisher, Mathematics
Colin Garnham

Managing Editor, Development
David Spiegel

Senior Program Manager
Shirley Barrett

Developmental Editor
Christy Hayhoe

Executive Managing Editor,
Special Projects
Cheryl Turner

Executive Managing Editor,
Production
Nicola Balfour

Senior Production Editor
Susan Skivington

Copyeditor
Susan McNish

Editorial Assistant
Amanda Davis

Senior Production Coordinator
Sharon Latta Paterson

Production Coordinator
Franca Mandarino

Creative Director
Angela Cluer

Art Director
Ken Phipps

Art Management
ArtPlus Ltd., Suzanne Peden

Illustrators
ArtPlus Ltd.

Interior and Cover Design
Suzanne Peden

Cover Image
Ko Fujiwara/Photonica

Composition
Nelson Gonzalez

Library and Archives Canada
Cataloguing in Publication

Nelson mathematics 8.
Workbook / Zimmer ... [et al.].

ISBN 13: 978-0-17-626996-8
ISBN 10: 0-17-626996-7

1. Mathematics—Problems,
exercises, etc..

I. Zimmer, David II. Title. III. Nelson
mathematics eight.

QA107.2.N448 2005 Suppl. 3
510   C2005-903593-5

Contents

Message to Parent/Guardian

This workbook contains questions for each lesson in your child's textbook *Nelson Mathematics 8*. The questions in the workbook are similar to the ones in the text, so they should look familiar to your child. The lesson Goal and the At-Home Help on each page will help you to provide support if your child needs it.

At the end of each chapter are two pages of multiple-choice questions called "Test Yourself." This is an opportunity for you and your child to see how well she or he understands.

You can help your child explore and understand math ideas by making available some commonly found materials, such as

- string, scissors, and a ruler (for measurement)
- counters such as bread tags, toothpicks, buttons, or coins (for number operations and patterns)
- packages, cans, toothpicks, and modelling clay (for geometry)
- grid paper, magazines, and newspapers (for data management)
- board game spinners, dice, and card games (for probability)

You might also encourage your child to use technology if it is available, such as

- a calculator (for exploring number patterns and operations)
- a computer (for investigating the wealth of information that exists on the Internet to help people learn and enjoy math)

Visit the Nelson Web site at **www.mathk8.nelson.com** to find out more about the mathematics your child is learning.

It's amazing what you can learn when you look at math through your child's eyes! Here are some things you might watch for.

Checklist
☑ Can your child clearly explain her or his thinking?
☑ Does your child check to see whether an answer makes sense?
☑ Does your child persevere until the work is complete?
☑ Does your child connect new concepts to what has already been learned?
☑ Is your child proud of what's been accomplished so far?

Identifying Prime and Composite Numbers

▶ **GOAL: Determine whether a number is prime or composite.**

1. List all prime numbers between 1 and 20.

_____

_____

2. 1 000 000 is not a prime number. How can you tell this by looking at it?

_____

_____

3. Identify each number as prime or composite. If the number is composite, list all of its factors.

    a) 21   **d)** 39

    b) 29   **e)** 51

    c) 33   **f)** 67

At-Home Help
A **prime number** is a number that has only two factors: 1 and itself. For example, 17 is a prime number because its only factors are 1 and 17.
A **composite number** is a number that has more than two factors. For example, 12 is a composite number because its factors are 1, 2, 3, 4, 6, and 12.
Use these divisibility rules to help you find the factors of a number.
• Numbers ending in 0 or 5 are divisible by 5.
• Numbers ending in 0 are divisible by 10.
• Even numbers are divisible by 2.
• If the sum of the digits in a number is divisible by 3, then the number itself is divisible by 3.

4. A park has the dimensions 17 m by 11 m.

    a) Is the area of the park a prime number? _____

    b) How can you tell without calculating the area of the park?

_____

_____

_____

1.2 Prime Factorization

▶ **GOAL: Express a composite number as the product of prime factors.**

1. A factor tree shows the factors of a number. Fill in the missing factors in each factor tree. Then list the prime factors of the number on the line to the right.

   a)
   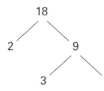

   _____

   b)
   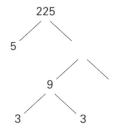

   _____

   > **At-Home Help**
   >
   > **Prime factorization** is a representation of a composite number as the product of its prime factors. For example, the prime factorization of 24 is $24 = 2 \times 2 \times 2 \times 3$, or $2^3 \times 3$. Usually the prime numbers are written in order from least to greatest.

2. Determine the prime factorization of each number.

   a) 95   b) 112   c) 164   d) 150

3. Determine the missing number in each prime factorization.

   a) $80 = \underline{\quad} \times 2 \times 2 \times 2 \times 5$ e) $4968 = 2^3 \times 3^3 \times \underline{\quad}$

   b) $198 = 2 \times 3 \times \underline{\quad} \times 11$ f) $297 = \underline{\quad}^3 \times 11$

   c) $1750 = 2 \times 5^3 \times \underline{\quad}$ g) $2639 = 7 \times \underline{\quad} \times 29$

   d) $665 = \underline{\quad} \times 7 \times 19$ h) $1331 = 11^{\underline{\quad}}$

4. 119 is the product of two prime numbers. Draw a factor tree for 119.

5. 6859 is equal to a prime number cubed. Draw a factor tree for 6859.

1.3 Common Factors and Common Multiples

▶ **GOAL:** Use the prime factorization to identify common factors and common multiples.

1. Find the GCF and the LCM of each pair of numbers. The first one is done for you.

   a) $54 = 2 \times 3 \times 3 \times 3$

   $81 = 3 \times 3 \times 3 \times 3$

   GCF: The common prime factors are 3, 3, and 3. Multiply these together to find the GCF, 27.

   LCM: Multiply the common prime factors (3, 3, and 3) with the prime factors that are not common (2 and 3) to get (3 x 3 x 3) x (2 x 3) = 162. The LCM is 162.

   b) $75 = 3 \times 5 \times 5$

   $250 = 2 \times 5 \times 5 \times 5$

   d) $100 = 2 \times 2 \times 5 \times 5$

   $210 = 2 \times 3 \times 5 \times 7$

   c) $80 = 2 \times 2 \times 2 \times 2 \times 5$

   $120 = 2 \times 2 \times 2 \times 3 \times 5$

   e) $50 = 2 \times 5 \times 5$

   $150 = 2 \times 3 \times 5 \times 5$

2. Use the prime factorization of each pair of numbers to identify three common factors and three common multiples.

   a) 14 and 84

   c) 48 and 72

   b) 50 and 350

   d) 24 and 132

3. Find the GCF and LCM of each pair of numbers.

   a) 15 and 90   c) 36 and 126

   b) 25 and 70   d) 63 and 84

4. Jordan and Manuel are on the track-and-field team at school. Running around the track one day, Jordan ran 444 m and Manuel ran 777 m. They both ran a whole number of times around the track. How far around is the track?

5. Tamara paid $3.00 for cartons of milk. Teo paid $3.75 for a different number of cartons at the same store.

   a) How much is one carton of milk?

   b) How many cartons did each person buy?

6. To practise for a tournament, Jordan bought 12 tennis balls and Annika bought 16. The tennis balls come in packages. Each package has the same number. What is the greatest possible number of tennis balls in each package?

7. Susan and Teo play soccer. Susan's team plays every five days. Teo's team plays every six days. When will the teams play on the same day?

1.4 Calculating Powers

▶ **GOAL: Represent and calculate numbers expressed as powers.**

1. Identify the base and the exponent for each power.

   a) 3^7 Base: _____   Exponent: _____

   b) 10^8 Base: _____   Exponent: _____

   c) 1^3 Base: _____   Exponent: _____

2. Write each power as repeated multiplication.

   a) $7^3 =$ _____

   b) $12^5 =$ _____

   c) $4^6 =$ _____

   d) $25^4 =$ _____

3. Write each multiplication as a power.

   a) $2 \times 2 \times 2 \times 2 \times 2 \times 2 \times 2 \times 2 \times 2 =$ _____

   b) $9 \times 9 \times 9 \times 9 =$ _____

   c) $21 \times 21 \times 21 \times 21 \times 21 =$ _____

   d) $103 \times 103 \times 103 \times 103 \times 103 \times 103 =$ _____

4. Write the following in symbols, then evaluate.

   a) 3 squared = _____

   b) 2 cubed = _____

   c) 5 squared = _____

   d) 4 cubed = _____

   e) 3 to the exponent 4 = _____

   f) 2 to the exponent 5 = _____

5. Calculate each power.

   a) $3^7 =$ _____

   b) $9^4 =$ _____

   c) $12^4 =$ _____

   d) $5^8 =$ _____

   e) $0.5^5 =$ _____

   f) $0.77^3 =$ _____

   g) $6.3^2 =$ _____

   h) $20.5^3 =$ _____

6. Write each power as repeated multiplication, and calculate.

   a) 0.7^4

   c) 1.3^2

   b) 11^3

   d) 99^4

7. Write each multiplication as a power, and calculate.

   a) $4 \times 4 \times 4 \times 4$

   c) $13 \times 13 \times 13$

   b) $6 \times 6 \times 6 \times 6 \times 6 \times 6$

   d) $3 \times 3 \times 3 \times 3 \times 3 \times 3 \times 3$

8. Write > or < to make each number sentence true.

   a) 2^3 _____ 3^2
   d) 3^4 _____ 4^3
   g) 5^3 _____ 3^5

   b) 1^2 _____ 2^1
   e) 4^5 _____ 5^4
   h) 2^6 _____ 6^2

   c) 10^2 _____ 2^{10}
   f) 3^6 _____ 6^3
   i) 1^5 _____ 5^1

9. Manuel tore a piece of paper into three parts. He tore each part into three more parts. If Manuel repeated this action 12 times in total, how many pieces of paper would he have?

10. A box holds nine smaller boxes. Each of the smaller boxes holds nine plastic containers. Each of the plastic containers holds nine bags. Each bag holds nine elastic bands. How many elastic bands are in the largest box?

11. Mars is about 7^{10} km from the sun. Saturn is about 7^{11} km from the sun. About how many times the distance from the sun to Mars is the distance from the sun to Saturn?

1.5 Expanded Form and Scientific Notation

▶ **GOAL: Express and compare numbers using expanded form and scientific notation.**

1. Fill in the blanks to express each number in scientific notation.

 a) $821 = 8.21 \times 10^{\underline{}}$

 b) $4385 = 4.385 \times 10^{\underline{}}$

 c) $625.7 = 6.257 \times 10^{\underline{}}$

 d) $8\ 500\ 000 = 8.5 \times 10^{\underline{}}$

2. Fill in each blank with the correct number.

 a) $847 = 8 \times \underline{} + 4 \times \underline{} + 7 \times \underline{}$

 b) $4956 = 4 \times \underline{} + 9 \times \underline{} + 5 \times \underline{} +$
    $6 \times \underline{}$

 c) $208 = \underline{} \times 10^2 + \underline{} \times 10 + \underline{} \times 1$

 d) $\underline{} = 4 \times 10^2 + 3 \times 10$

At-Home Help

Scientific notation is a way of writing a number as a decimal between 1 and 10 multiplied by a power of 10. For example, 70 120 is written as 7.012×10^4.

In a TI-15 calculator, you can enter the number 1.81×10^{11} like this: 1.81 [×] 10 [^] 11 [=]

The calculator will display the number like this:

$(1.81 \times 10^{\wedge}11)$

Expanded form is a way of writing a number that shows the value of each digit as a power of 10. For example, 1209 in expanded form is $1 \times 10^3 + 2 \times 10^2 + 0 \times 10^1 + 9 \times 1$. You can also leave out the zeros and write $1 \times 10^3 + 2 \times 10^2 + 9 \times 1$.

3. Fill in the blanks in the chart.

	Standard form	Expanded form	Scientific notation
a)	250	$2 \times 10^2 + 5 \times 10$	2.5×10^2
b)		$3 \times 10^3 + 4 \times 10^2 + 8 \times 10 + 1 \times 1$	
c)			7.11×10^3
d)	9854		
e)			8.803×10^4
f)	10 772		
g)		$1 \times 10^5 + 9 \times 10^3 + 5 \times 1$	
h)			6.03×10^4

4. Write < or > to make each number sentence true.

 a) 4.2×10^2 _____ 5000

 b) $3 \times 10^5 + 2 \times 10 + 4 \times 1$ _____ 49 877

 c) 7.73×10^4 _____ $6 \times 10^3 + 5 \times 10^2 + 7 \times 1$

1.6 Square Roots

▶ **GOAL:** Estimate and calculate the square root of a whole number.

1. Use mental math to calculate each square root.

   a) $\sqrt{9}$ = _____

   b) $\sqrt{25}$ = _____

   c) $\sqrt{49}$ = _____

   d) $\sqrt{64}$ = _____

   e) $\sqrt{81}$ = _____

   f) $\sqrt{121}$ = _____

   g) $\sqrt{400}$ = _____

   h) $\sqrt{3600}$ = _____

2. Estimate each square root to one decimal place. The first one is done for you.

   a) $\sqrt{15}$

   $3 \times 3 = 9$, and $4 \times 4 = 16$, so $3.9 \times 3.9 \approx 15$

   $\sqrt{15} \doteq 3.9$

   (The $\doteq$ symbol means "approximately equal.")

   b) $\sqrt{65}$

   c) $\sqrt{24}$

   d) $\sqrt{102}$

   e) $\sqrt{10}$

   f) $\sqrt{35}$

> ## At-Home Help
>
> A **square root** is one of two equal factors of a number. For example, the square root of 100 is represented as $\sqrt{100}$ and is equal to 10, because 10×10 or $10^2 = 100$.
>
> If you have a TI-15 calculator, use this key sequence to calculate the square root of 100:
>
> ☑100 ⟮ =
>
> If you have a different kind of calculator, use this key sequence:
>
> 100 ☑

3. Calculate each square root using a calculator. Round to three decimal places.

   a) $\sqrt{19}$ = _____

   b) $\sqrt{33}$ = _____

   c) $\sqrt{85}$ = _____

   d) $\sqrt{138}$ = _____

   e) $\sqrt{737}$ = _____

   f) $\sqrt{488}$ = _____

4. A square field has an area of 625 m². What are its dimensions?

1.7 Exploring Square Roots and Squares

▶ **GOAL:** Determine the diagonal lengths, side lengths, and areas of squares.

1. **a)** What is the side length of the square below?

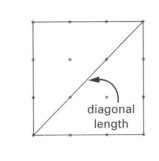

diagonal length

> **At-Home Help**
>
> You can find the diagonal length of a square using this formula:
>
> Diagonal length = (side length) $\sqrt{2}$

b) Calculate the area of the square.

c) Calculate the diagonal length of the square. Round your answer to three decimal places.

2. Calculate the area for each square with the dimensions given.

   a) 6 cm by 6 cm   **b)** 8 m by 8 m   **c)** 11 cm by 11 cm

3. Use a calculator to find the diagonal length of each square in question 2. Round your answers to three decimal places.

   a)   **b)**   **c)**

4. Calculate the side length of each square with the area given.

   a) 49 cm^2 **b)** 144 cm^2 **c)** 225 m^2

5. Use a calculator to find the diagonal length of each square in question 4. Round your answers to three decimal places.

   a)   **b)**   **c)**

Order of Operations

▶ **GOAL: Apply the rules for order of operations to whole numbers and decimals.**

1. Selena and Nathan were asked to evaluate $5 \times 1 + 2 \times (3 - 1)$. They each got a different answer.

   Selena's Solution

   $$5 \times 1 + 2 \times (3 - 1) = 5 + 2 \times (3 - 1)$$
   $$= 7 \times (3 - 1)$$
   $$= 7 \times 2$$
   $$= 14$$

   Nathan's Solution

   $$5 \times 1 + 2 \times (3 - 1) = 5 \times 3 \times (3 - 1)$$
   $$= 15 \times (3 - 1)$$
   $$= 15 \times 2$$
   $$= 30$$

   a) What was Selena's error?

   _____

   b) What was Nathan's error?

   _____

   c) Solve the problem.

   At-Home Help

   You can use the memory aid **BEDMAS** to remember the rules for order of operations.

   Brackets

   Exponents and square roots

   Divide and **M**ultiply from left to right

   Add and **S**ubtract from left to right

   Here are some additional tips to help you.

   - If there is more than one set of brackets, do the calculations in the inner brackets first.
   - If a square root sign covers an expression, do the calculations inside the square root first.

2. Place brackets to make each equation true.

   a) $5 - 1 \times 6 = 24$

   b) $12 \div 4 - 1 = 4$

   c) $3 + 4 \times 6 - 5 = 7$

   d) $6 + 8 \div 2 = 7$

   e) $1 + 2^2 = 9$

   f) $20 - 3 \times 2 + 5 = 9$

3. Evaluate each expression. Show your work.

   a) $(6 + 5) \times (7 - 3)$

   b) $2^3 + 3^2$

   c) $(7 - 3)^2 + (7 + 1)^2$

   d) $1^2 + 2^2 + 3^2 + 4^4$

   e) $(1 + 2 + 3 + 4)^2$

   f) $\sqrt{2 + 7}$

4. Evaluate each expression. Show your work.

   a) $5^2 - \sqrt{25}$

   e) $3 \times 4 - 3 \div 2 + 2$

   b) $9 \times 8 - 7^2$

   f) $(1 + 5 + 3)^2 \times (4 \times 2 - 7)$

   c) $100 - [(2 + 3) \times (1 + 4)]$

   g) $(2^2 + 6) - \sqrt{70 - 6}$

   d) $\sqrt{(2 + 3) \times (1 + 4)}$

   h) $[2 \times (5 + 4)] \div \sqrt{36}$

5. The teacher has 15 gold prize ribbons, 22 blue ribbons, and 53 red ribbons. There are 12 boys and 18 girls in the class. If the teacher divides the ribbons evenly among the students, how many ribbons will each student have? Write an expression using brackets, then solve your expression to find the answer.

6. For the bake sale, Sandra baked 4 trays of cookies, with 12 cookies on each tray. Teo baked 6 pans of brownies and divided each pan into 8 pieces. How many items will Sandra and Teo have for sale in total? Write a mathematical expression, then solve your expression to find the answer.

1.9 Communicating about Number Problems

▶ **GOAL: Explain how to create and solve problems that involve numbers.**

1. Solve each problem. Use the Communication Checklist to help you explain your solution.

   a) Earth is 149 597 890 km from the sun. The planet Pluto is about 39.5 times farther away from the sun than Earth. How far is Pluto from the sun? Round your answer to three digits and express it in scientific notation.

At-Home Help

Use this Communication Checklist to help you create and solve number problems.

Communication Checklist
☑ Did you identify the given information?
☑ Did you show how to solve your problem step by step?
☑ Did you explain your method of calculation?
☑ Did you explain why each calculation is reasonable?

   b) On the planet Jupiter, one day is equal to 9.925 h on Earth. How many minutes are there in one week on Jupiter? Express your answer in scientific notation.

2. Earth's mass is 5 973 700 000 000 000 000 000 000 kg.

   a) Express this number using scientific notation. _____

   b) The mass of Earth is about 81 times greater than the mass of the moon. What is the moon's mass? Round your answer to five digits.

3. Use some of the numbers below as well as other numbers you need to create a problem. Solve your problem and explain your solution.

   The moon is about 384 400 km from Earth.

   A typical car travels at about 100 km/h.

Test Yourself

1. Identify each number as prime or composite or neither. If a number is composite, list all its factors.

   a) 1

   b) 7

   c) 21

   d) 85

   e) 19

   f) 38

2. Determine the prime factorization of each number.

   a) 78

   b) 675

   c) 1092

   d) 660

   e) 567

   f) 1372

3. Use prime factorization to find the GCF and LCM of each pair of numbers.

   a) 12 and 33

   c) 80 and 220

   b) 18 and 42

   d) 19 and 15

4. Write each expression as a power, and calculate. Round your answers to three decimal places where needed.

   a) $9 \times 9 \times 9 =$ _____

   b) $3 \times 3 \times 3 \times 3 \times 3 \times 3 \times 3 =$ _____

   c) $0.5 \times 0.5 \times 0.5 \times 0.5 =$ _____

   d) $5.3 \times 5.3 \times 5.3 \times 5.3 \times 5.3 \times 5.3 =$ _____

5. Write each power as repeated multiplication, and calculate. Round your answers to three decimal places where needed.

   a) $2^8 =$ _____

   b) $4^4 =$ _____

   c) $8.1^5 =$ _____

   d) $7^9 =$ _____

6. Express each number in expanded form.

a) 8884 = _____

_____

b) 19 203 = _____

_____

c) 2.2×10^4 = _____

_____

7. Express each number in scientific notation.

a) 732 = _____

b) 9404 = _____

c) $8 \times 10^4 + 4 \times 10^3 + 9 \times 10^2 + 1 \times 10 + 4 \times 1$ =

_____

d) $1 \times 10^6 + 7 \times 10^5 + 3 \times 10^4 + 2 \times 10$ = _____

8. Write < or > to make each expression true.

a) 707 000 _____ 4.1322×10^4

b) 33 992 _____ $1 \times 10^3 + 2 \times 10^2 + 4 \times 10 + 5 \times 1$

c) 9.202×10^7 _____ $8 \times 10^5 + 2 \times 10^4 + 7 \times 10^3 + 1 \times 10^2 + 2 \times 10 + 9 \times 1$

d) 1.5×10^5 _____ $7 \times 10^4 + 9 \times 10^3 + 2 \times 10^2 + 5 \times 10 + 3 \times 1$

9. Estimate each square root to one decimal place.

a) $\sqrt{35}$ **c)** $\sqrt{5}$

b) $\sqrt{26}$ **d)** $\sqrt{11}$

10. Calculate.

a) $\sqrt{15}$ **c)** $\sqrt{504}$

b) $\sqrt{44}$ **d)** $\sqrt{2280}$

11. The surface area of the moon is 37 932 330 km². Calculate the side length of a square with the same area. Show your work.

12. Calculate the expressions below.

a) $3 \times 8 + 2 - 11$

b) $4^2 - 2^3$

c) $(2 + 7) \times (9 + 3)$

d) $(19 - 8 + 4)^3$

e) $[(2 + 8) \times 3] + 5$

f) $(3 + 4 + 1)^2 \div 2^4$

g) $\sqrt{11 - 5 + 3}$

h) $22 - \sqrt{6^2 \times 4}$

2.1 Expressing Fractions as Decimals

▶ **GOAL: Use division to express fractions as decimals.**

1. Write each repeating decimal using bar notation.

   a) 0.666 666 666... = _____

   b) 0.090 909 09... = _____

   c) 0.142 853 714 285 37... = _____

2. Divide each numerator by its denominator to convert the fractions into decimals. Which fractions have repeating decimal equivalents?

   a) $\frac{1}{6}$ = _____

   b) $\frac{3}{10}$ = _____

   c) $\frac{2}{7}$ = _____

   d) $\frac{8}{11}$ = _____

3. Write < or > to make each expression true.

   a) $\frac{3}{5}$ ____ $\frac{7}{10}$

   b) $\frac{1}{3}$ ____ $\frac{3}{8}$

   c) $\frac{10}{11}$ ____ $\frac{19}{20}$

   d) $\frac{4}{5}$ ____ $\frac{7}{9}$

   e) $\frac{1}{13}$ ____ $\frac{3}{31}$

   f) $\frac{3}{200}$ ____ $\frac{1}{77}$

4. Predict which fractions are equivalent to a terminating or repeating decimal. Use a calculator to check your predictions.

   a) $\frac{1}{5}$

   b) $\frac{8}{9}$

   c) $\frac{2}{13}$

   d) $\frac{3}{25}$

   e) $\frac{6}{11}$

   f) $\frac{7}{100}$

   g) $\frac{2}{85}$

   h) $\frac{9}{40}$

   i) $\frac{23}{300}$

2.2 Multiplying and Dividing Decimals

▶ **GOAL: Understand and apply multiplication and division of decimals.**

1. The digits for each answer are shown. Estimate to place the decimal point.

   a) $3.6 \times 4 = 144$

   b) $4.2 \times 2.2 = 924$

   c) $11.1 \times 3.5 = 3885$

   d) $47.5 \times 3.7 = 17575$

   e) $4.3 \div 0.01 = 430$

   f) $27.4 \div 10.5 = 260\ 952\ 381$

2. Calculate.

   a) $0.7 \times 0.5 =$ _____

   b) $2.37 \times 14 =$ _____

   c) $15 \times 0.14 =$ _____

   d) $0.41 \times 0.21 =$ _____

   e) $0.23 \times 1.4 =$ _____

   f) $15 \times 3.2 =$ _____

   g) $1.7 \times 3.23 =$ _____

   h) $14.8 \times 12.39 =$ _____

3. Calculate.

   a) $2.7 \div 3 =$ _____

   b) $1.6 \div 4 =$ _____

   c) $3.5 \div 5 =$ _____

   d) $0.48 \div 6 =$ _____

   e) $8.19 \div 2.1 =$ _____

   f) $12.32 \div 7.7 =$ _____

   g) $25.3 \div 4.6 =$ _____

   h) $146.32 \div 11.8 =$ _____

4. Nathan worked for 13.5 h at $9.75 per hour. How much money did he make?

5. Cooking oil costs $5.89/kg. How much oil is there if the total cost is $17.92?

6. It takes 0.45 kg of clay to make one figurine. How many figurines can be made from 12.75 kg of clay?

7. Two fishing records were set in Canada:
   - Ken Fraser caught a tuna with a mass of 678.6 kg at Auld Cove.
   - Larry Daunis caught a lake trout with a mass of 29.5 kg in Great Bear Lake.

   a) Based on the records above, which fish has the greater mass: 100 lake trout or 4 tuna?

   b) Calculate the masses in part (a). How reasonable was your estimate?

8. Annika, Tamara, and Susan are buying supplies for a party. Annika spends $15.95, Tamara $18.46, and Susan $22.80. They are dividing up the expenses equally.

   a) How much money should Annika give Susan?

   b) How much money should Tamara give Susan?

9. A grocery store used to sell bulk chocolate chip cookies for $0.65 for 100 g. The price increased by $0.05 for 100 g. What is the new price for 400 g of bulk chocolate chip cookies?

10. Duck Mountain Provincial Park is on the boundary of Saskatchewan and Manitoba. To visit the sites, Nathan's family drove 6.8 km, 9.8 km, 20.3 km, and 46.8 km. If they drove for 4.5 h, what was their average speed?

2.3 Exploring Ratios

▶ **GOAL: Investigate the ratios of areas created by pattern block designs.**

1. Write a ratio for each set of squares that compares the number of grey squares to the number of white squares.

a)    Ratio: _____

b) 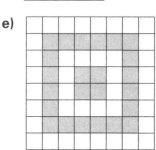   Ratio: _____

c)   Ratio: _____

d)   Ratio: _____

e)   Ratio: _____

2. Teo has four pairs of white socks, two pairs of yellow socks, one pair of green socks, and three pairs of black socks.

   a) What is the ratio of white socks to black socks? _____

   b) What is the ratio of green socks to black socks? _____

   c) What is the ratio of yellow socks to white socks? _____

   d) What is the ratio of black socks to yellow socks to green socks? _____

3. Use two different colours of pencil to draw a pattern in the grid below that matches the ratio 12 : 4.

2.4 Ratios

▶ **GOAL: Solve problems that involve ratios.**

1. Fill in the missing terms.

   a) 1:2 = ____ : 4   d) 1:5 = 3:____

   b) 1:____ = 3:6   e) ____:6 = 1:3

   c) 3:5 = ____ : 10   f) 9:15 = ____:5

2. What is the scale factor in each proportion?

   a) 1:2 = 5:10   Scale factor: _____

   b) 5:6 = 10:12   Scale factor: _____

   c) 4:5 = 24:30   Scale factor: _____

   d) 3:7 = 30:70   Scale factor: _____

3. Fill in the missing terms, and write the scale factor.

   a) 3:5:1 = 6:____:2   Scale factor: _____

   b) 3:4:3 = 15:20:____   Scale factor: _____

   c) 8:3 = 4:____   Scale factor: _____

   d) 2.1:4:7.7 = ____:12:23.1   Scale factor: _____

   e) 16:1:____ = ____:0.125:3   Scale factor: _____

   f) 5.2:____:____ = 16.64:14.72:28.8   Scale factor: _____

4. Annika's flight to Ottawa took 45 min. The bus ride to the airport took 3 h. Write a ratio to compare the time on the bus to the time on the plane.

5. In Allanville, 5 out of every 6 homes recycle bottles. There are 48 homes in the area. How many homes recycle bottles?

6. When the pedal on a bike has turned 3 times in fourth gear, the rear wheel has turned 7 times. When the pedal has turned 12 times, how many times has the rear wheel turned?

Rates

▶ **GOAL: Determine and apply rates to solve problems.**

1. Calculate the equivalent unit rate.

   a) $85.50 earned in 7 h = _____

   b) $76.00 for six CDs = _____

   c) 120 km in 10 h = _____

   d) 30 m in 0.5 s = _____

   e) six bottles of juice for $2.40 = _____

   f) $399 earned in three weeks = _____

   g) three cans of soup for $2.25 = _____

   h) 400 km in 5 h = _____

   i) $42.80 for 5.5 kg = _____

2. Yesterday, Tamara's older sister earned $90 during an 8 h shift.

   a) How much did she earn each hour?

   b) How much will she earn in a 40 h week?

3. Pedro built nine bicycles in 25 h. At this rate, how many bicycles will he build in a 40 h week?

4. Jordan can type 96 words in 2 min. How many words can she type in 5 min?

5. Teo earns $47.25 in 7 h of work at Beck's Hamburgers. How much will he earn in 12 h?

6. The most intense rainfall on record was 75 mm in 2 min at Barst, Guadeloupe. At this rate, how much rain would you expect to fall in 1 h?

2.6 Representing Percent

▶ **GOAL:** Represent and calculate percents that involve whole numbers or decimals, and whole number percents that are greater than 100%.

1. What percent is represented by the shaded part of the diagram?

a)

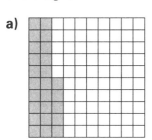

Percent: _____

b)

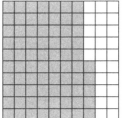

Percent: _____

d)

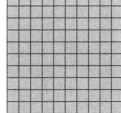

Percent: _____

c)

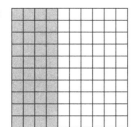

Percent: _____

e)

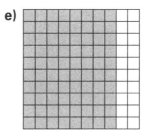

Percent: _____

2. What percent is represented by the unshaded part of each diagram in question 1?

a) Percent: _____

b) Percent: _____

c) Percent: _____

d) Percent: _____

e) Percent: _____

3. Jordan's dance school has 340 pupils. Eighty percent (80%) of the pupils are under 15 years old. Use the grid and the information below to help you answer the questions. The grid represents 100%, so one square represents:

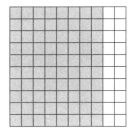

340 ÷ 100 = 3.4 pupils.

a) How many pupils are under 15? _____

b) How many pupils are over 15? _____

4. Use the grids provided to model and calculate.

a) 15% of $100 = _____

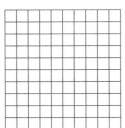

c) 65% of $170 = _____

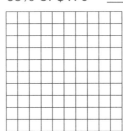

b) 80% of $40 = _____

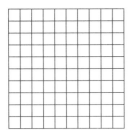

d) 170% of $200 = _____

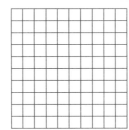

5. Susan had 30 items of clothing in her wardrobe. She donated 20% of her clothing during a charity clothing drive at the school. How many items of clothing did Susan donate?

6. Teo invited 14 friends to his birthday party. At the party, there were 5 pizzas, 2 tubs of ice cream, 45 cupcakes, and 8 bags of popcorn. Calculate how much of each food was eaten.

a) 80% of the pizza   c) 60% of the cupcakes

b) 50% of the ice cream   d) 75% of the popcorn

Solving Percent Problems

▶ **GOAL: Use proportions to solve percent problems.**

1. Calculate the missing term in each proportion.

   a) $\dfrac{\blacksquare}{100} = \dfrac{2}{8}$ d) $\dfrac{14}{100} = \dfrac{\blacksquare}{300}$

   b) $\dfrac{\blacksquare}{100} = \dfrac{96}{128}$ e) $\dfrac{24}{100} = \dfrac{6}{\blacksquare}$

   c) $\dfrac{20}{100} = \dfrac{\blacksquare}{5}$ f) $\dfrac{75}{100} = \dfrac{9}{\blacksquare}$

2. Out of 500 students interviewed, 325 said they had too much homework. What percent of students said they had too much homework?

3. Of 45 people in the room, 27 were women. What percent were women?

4. Susan has 240 CDs. If 35% of them are jazz, how many jazz CDs does she have?

5. Ken was at bat 120 times during the baseball season. If he hit the ball 15% of the time, how many times did he have a hit?

6. Selena picked eight baskets of tomatoes. Her sister threw away one of the baskets due to bruising. What percent were good?

At-Home Help

You can use proportions to solve percent problems. For example, to find 40% of 90, follow these steps:

- First, write a proportion.

  $\dfrac{\blacksquare}{100} = \dfrac{\text{part}}{\text{whole}}$

  $\dfrac{40}{100} = \dfrac{\blacksquare}{90}$

- Next, find the scale factor.

  $\dfrac{40}{100} = \dfrac{\blacksquare}{90}$

  $\times 0.9$

- Use the scale factor to find the missing term:

  $\dfrac{40 \times 0.9}{100 \times 0.9} = \dfrac{36}{90}$

The answer is 36.

---

7. A macaroni and cheese dish had 250 g of macaroni and 45 g of cheese. What percent of the dish was cheese?

8. Tamara has completed 60% of her practice time for the track meet. If she is expected to practise for 18 h, how long has she already practised?

9. The total length of the Trans-Canada Highway is 7870 km. About 6% of the highway is in Alberta. How many kilometres are in Alberta?

10. Of all the bolts in a box, 1% are defective. There are 62 defective bolts. How many bolts in total are in the box?

11. Annika needs five cards to complete her collection. If this is 10% of the total collection, how many cards are in the set?

12. Selena hit 20% of the pitches thrown to her. If she had eight hits, how many pitches were thrown?

13. Annika earned $375 from her summer job. Ken earned 160% of the amount Annika earned. How much did Ken earn?

14. A shirt is on sale for 25% off. If the original price was $120, what is the sale price?

2.8 Solving Percent Problems Using Decimals

▶ **GOAL: Use percents to solve problems that involve everyday situations.**

1. Nathan's brother bought a used car. The original price of the car was $3075.66. He was given a 6% discount. How much was the discount?

2. Calculate the interest paid for each amount in one year.

	Amount	Rate of interest	Interest paid
a)	$150.00	3% per year	
b)	$250.00	8% per year	
c)	$325.00	7.5% per year	
d)	$422.50	6.5% per year	

3. Sandra's lunch came to $12.84 plus 15% tax. What was the total cost of her lunch?

4. Swimsuits sell regularly for $44.95. Calculate the price of a swimsuit, given each discount.

a) 10% off

b) 75% off

5. Selena bought a TV for her bedroom. The original price was $299.99, but she bought it on sale for 30% off. Selena also paid 15% tax. How much money did she spend on the TV?

Solve Problems by Changing Your Point of View

▶ **GOAL: Solve problems by looking at situations in different ways.**

1. a) Nathan wants to find the sale price of a $30 shirt at 20% off. He performs these calculations:

100% − 20% = 80% or 0.80
$30 × 0.80 = $24

Explain Nathan's reasoning.

_____

_____

_____

b) Jordan wants to find the purchase price of a $95 dress at 10% off with 15% tax. She performs these calculations:

100% − 10% = 90% or 0.90
100% + 15% = 115% or 1.15
$95.00 × 0.90 × 1.15 = $98.33

Explain Jordan's reasoning.

_____

_____

_____

_____

2. Use a "change-your-point-of-view" strategy to solve each problem.

a) A coat is on sale for 60% off. The original price was $325.75. What is the sale price?

b) A pair of shoes cost $88.50. Ken bought them for 35% off, plus 15% tax. How much did he pay?

Test Yourself

1. Write each fraction as a terminating decimal.

   a) $\dfrac{1}{4}$ = _____

   b) $\dfrac{7}{10}$ = _____

   c) $\dfrac{3}{8}$ = _____

   d) $\dfrac{17}{50}$ = _____

   e) $\dfrac{9}{16}$ = _____

   f) $\dfrac{53}{64}$ = _____

2. Write each fraction as a repeating decimal.

   a) $\dfrac{2}{3}$ = _____

   b) $\dfrac{6}{7}$ = _____

   c) $\dfrac{1}{12}$ = _____

   d) $\dfrac{5}{9}$ = _____

   e) $\dfrac{19}{21}$ = _____

   f) $\dfrac{4}{11}$ = _____

3. Use prime factorization to determine whether each fraction is equivalent to a terminating or a repeating decimal.

   a) $\dfrac{1}{8}$

   b) $\dfrac{5}{6}$

   c) $\dfrac{11}{14}$

   d) $\dfrac{7}{20}$

   e) $\dfrac{17}{100}$

   f) $\dfrac{8}{13}$

4. Calculate.

   a) $2.2 \times 4 =$ _____

   b) $5.1 \times 6.3 =$ _____

   c) $12.7 \times 0.3 =$ _____

   d) $5.5 \div 4 =$ _____

   e) $7.4 \div 0.128 =$ _____

   f) $0.028 \div 0.64 =$ _____

5. Teo worked for 42.5 h at $7.75 per hour. How much did he earn?

6. Fill in the missing terms in each proportion.

   a) $5 : 2 = 10 :$ ____

   b) $6 : 1 =$ ____ $: 5$

   c) $12 :$ ____ $= 4 : 3$

   d) $1 : 2 : 3 =$ ____ $:$ ____ $: 6$

   e) $7 :$ ____ $: 5 = 21 : 9 :$ ____

   f) ____ $: 5 : 35 = 4 : 1 :$ ____

7. Susan's mom runs at an average of 5.4 km/h. How far can she run in 3.2 h?

8. Calculate the unit cost.

   a) $8.40 for three hamburgers

   b) $19.50 for ten cans of soup

   c) $34.25 for two shirts

   d) $740.12 for 28.5 m of steel cable

   e) $63.80 for 18.3 kg of flour

   f) $23 745.04 for four used cars

9. Jordan's recipe for chocolate cake asks for 2 c of flour, $\frac{1}{2}$ c of butter, and 1 c of sugar, among other ingredients. How much flour, butter, and sugar will she need to make three cakes?

10. There are 515 students in a school. How many students are in each category?

   a) 80% have a brother or sister in the school _____

   b) 47% are girls

   _____

   c) 66% are 13 years old or under

   _____

11. Calculate.

   a) 5% of 300 = _____

   b) $\frac{15}{16}$ = _____%

   c) 32% of _____ = 88

   d) 18% of 190 = _____

   e) $\frac{43}{50}$ = _____%

   f) 92.5% of _____ = 578.125

12. Twenty-five percent (25%) of Manuel's classmates went to the library last weekend. If there are 28 students in Manuel's class, how many were at the library?

13. Out of the 40 families in Selena's neighbourhood, 17 have cats. What percent of the families have a cat?

14. Ken's sister borrowed $530 from the bank at 8.4% per year.

   a) How much interest did she pay in one year?

   _____

   b) How much interest did she pay in three years?

   _____

15. You have a new job where you earn 13% commission in addition to $5.25 per hour. On your first day, you work for 7.75 h and sell $95.20 worth of merchandise. How much money did you make?

16. Calculate each price.

   a) a pair of roller blades for $275.80, on sale at 45% off

   b) a pair of shoes for $86.35, on sale at 62% off

3.1 Organizing and Presenting Data

▶ **GOAL: Organize and present data to solve problems and make decisions.**

1. Carina's community association is deciding whether to build a skateboard park (which could also be used for rollerblading) or a playing field. Carina interviewed students at her school and collected the data in the table below.

Number of students	Favourite sport
85	ultimate Frisbee
102	skateboarding
18	rugby
67	soccer
26	baseball
38	rollerblading

At-Home Help

Graphs are commonly used to organize and present data. Different types of graphs include
- bar graphs
- pictographs
- line graphs
- scatter plots
- stem-and-leaf plots
- circle graphs

a) Choose an appropriate type of graph. Construct a graph to display Carina's data.

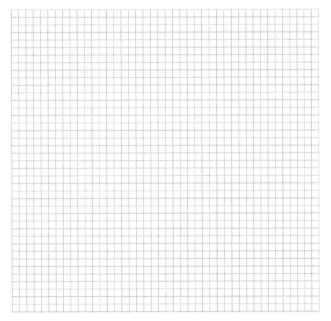

b) What percent of students prefer sports that take place in a field?

c) What percent of students prefer skateboarding or rollerblading?

d) Based on the data, should the association build a skateboard park or a playing field? Why?

3.2 Exploring Sample Size

▶ **GOAL: Explore how sample size represents a population.**

1. For each situation, explain why data is collected using a sample instead of taking a census.

   a) the quality control in the manufacture of microwave popcorn

   _____

   b) the percent of Canadian families with a computer

   _____

   c) the number of hours a light bulb will shine before burning out

   _____

2. Identify whether the data was gathered by taking a census or by using a sample.

   a) To determine whether students in portable 2 were showing any signs of environmental allergies to moulds, each student was interviewed.

   _____

   b) To determine the quality of printer cartridges, every 500th cartridge was tested. _____

   c) To determine if any eggs were broken, every package was opened.

   _____

   d) To determine what Canadian families prefer as a family vacation, selected households were telephoned. _____

   e) To determine whether taxpayers wanted a new community pool, a questionnaire was enclosed in 20% of the tax bills.

   _____

3. To gather data about the following, would you take a census or use a sample? Explain your choice.

   a) the favourite CD of your class _____

   _____

   b) the life expectancy of the new "Ultra Battery" _____

   _____

3.3 Using Electronic Databases

▶ **GOAL: Use statistics software to display data from electronic databases, and use the data to solve problems.**

1. Construct a comparative bar graph that compares the number of visits to the U.S.A. with the sum of the number of visits to the other 11 countries. Use statistics software if you have access to it, or draw your graph on the grid below.

2. Are visits to the U.S.A. increasing or decreasing?

3. Are visits to other countries increasing or decreasing?

4. The top 12 countries were sorted according to the number of visits in 2000. What would the top 5 countries be if the database were sorted according to the number of visits in 2003?

5. What percent of the total number of visits in 2003 were to the U.S.A.?

6. What percent of the total number of visits in 2001 were to Japan?

Top 12 Countries Visited by Canadians

Country visited	Visits (hundred thousands)			
	2000	2001	2002	2003
U.S.A.	146.7	135.3	130.2	126.7
U.K.	8.0	6.7	7.2	6.8
Mexico	6.9	6.9	6.1	7.2
France	4.6	4.8	5.1	5.1
Germany	2.8	2.5	2.6	3.3
Cuba	2.6	3.5	3.3	5.0
Italy	2.3	2.3	2.5	2.5
Dominican Republic	1.9	2.5	3.2	4.2
Netherlands	1.6	1.5	1.6	1.6
Switzerland	1.5	1.4	1.2	1.2
Spain	1.4	1.6	1.5	1.5
Japan	1.2	1.2	1.2	1.2

[Data from Statistics Canada.]

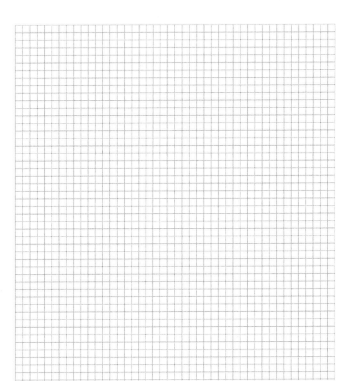

3.4 Histograms

▶ **GOAL:** Use histograms to describe appropriate data.

1. For each of the following, indicate whether you would use a bar graph or a histogram.

a) the finish times of 10 runners in a race

_____

b) the frequency of runners reaching the finish line each 30 min during an 8 h marathon

_____

c) the distribution of ages in the Canadian population as recorded in 2004

_____

d) the tonnes of material per year received at a recycling plant _____

e) the number of each colour of shoes sold in a store in one week _____

At-Home Help

A **histogram** is a graph with bars that shows frequencies for data organized into intervals. The intervals line up side-by-side, without gaps, on the number line.

Histograms and bar graphs are similar in that both are graphs with bars. The difference is that bar graphs are used to display specific data (such as the heights of 10 students in a class), while histograms are used to display intervals (such as the frequency of students with heights in the intervals 145−155 cm, 155−165 cm, and 165−175 cm).

2. The ages of the 36 members of the Lucca Swimming Club are given below.

```
25  47  38  15  42  36  34  52  18  26  53  45
41  22  49  41  32  19  28  44  36  63  47  22
47  31  34  17  49  24  55  37  46  21  46  39
```

a) Organize the data into the frequency table.

Age	10−20	20−30	30−40	40−50	50−60	60−70
Frequency						

b) Draw and label a histogram to show this distribution.

Ages of Lucca Swimming Club Members

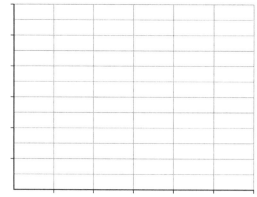

Frequency

Age (years)

3. Maria is practising for a bike race. She has been recording her time over a 2 km distance as she practises. Her times are given below, in minutes.

7.8 7.6 8.4 7.1 9.0 6.8 7.6 8.2

8.1 7.7 6.9 8.3 7.9 9.4 7.9 7.4

7.2 8.2 7.3 8.8 7.6 8.9 9.6 7.8

a) Fill in the frequency table for the data.

Time (min)	6.5−7.0	7.0−7.5	7.5−8.0	8.0−8.5	8.5−9.0	9.0−9.5	9.5+
Frequency							

b) Draw and label a histogram to display the data.

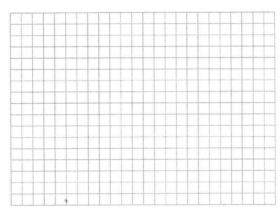

4. For a science project, Benjamin is growing seedlings from soy beans. He prepared a histogram to organize his data. Use Benjamin's histogram to answer the questions.

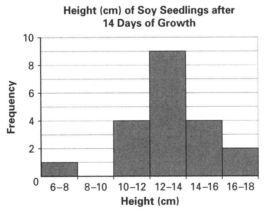

a) How many plants did Benjamin grow in total? _____

b) Can you use the histogram to find the height of the tallest plant? Why or why not? _____

c) If you grew several seedlings from soy beans, what height interval would they be most likely to grow to? Explain your answer.

_____

_____

Mean, Median, and Mode

▶ **GOAL: Use means, medians, and modes to compare groups of data.**

1. Determine the mean, median, and mode for each set of data. Round your answers to one decimal point when needed.

> **At-Home Help**
>
> The **mean** is the average, or the sum of a set of numbers divided by the number of numbers in the set.
>
> The **median** is the middle value in a set of ordered data. When there is an odd number of numbers, the median is the middle number. When there is an even number of numbers, the median is the mean of the two middle numbers.
>
> The **mode** is the number that occurs most often in a set of data; there can be more than one mode, or there might be no mode.

   a) 2, 5, 6, 8, 10, 12, 15

   Mean: _____

   Median: _____

   Mode: _____

   b) 3, 5, 5, 6, 12, 14

   Mean: _____

   Median: _____

   Mode: _____

   c) 9, 3, 3, 6, 1, 7, 2, 3

   Mean: _____

   Median: _____

   Mode: _____

   d) 15, 17, 14, 13, 19, 20, 11, 14, 15

   Mean: _____   Median: _____   Mode: _____

   e) 35, 36, 37, 31, 28, 43

   Mean: _____   Median: _____   Mode: _____

   f) 101, 104, 110, 98, 97, 120, 114, 116

   Mean: _____   Median: _____   Mode: _____

2. a) Determine the mean and median for the following set of data:

   1.5, 3.3, 4.6, 7.5, 8.2, 1.3, 9.0, 2.4, 1.7, 3.4, 4.7

   Mean: _____   Median: _____

   b) Remove the greatest and least values. Determine the mean and median. Which changed the most?

   Mean: _____   Median: _____

3. Rowyn did a survey to discover the ages of the people who live on her block. She obtained the following data:

23 27   2   1   4 65 64 46 43 18 15 34
12   9 83 38 41 13 74 31 26   5   7   8

Stem	Leaf

  a) Fill in the stem-and-leaf plot to organize and display Rowyn's data.

  b) Determine the mean and median.

   Mean: _____   Median: _____

  c) Shortly after Rowyn did her survey, the oldest member on the block went to live with her daughter in another city. Determine the new mean and median.

   Mean: _____   Median: _____

  d) Which measure changed the most? Explain.

   _____

4. The number of people attending the Sunnydale Tennis Club each week for 10 weeks is shown. Determine the mean, median, and mode.

18   15   23   12   20   26   14   17   22   20

Mean: _____   Median: _____   Mode: _____

5. a) If the mean of a set of data is 23, must 23 be one of the data values? Use an example to back up your answer.

   _____

   _____

  b) Construct a set of data whose mean is one of the data values.

   _____

  c) Construct a set of data whose mean is not one of the data values.

   _____

6. a) If the median of a set of data is 23, must 23 be one of the data values? Use an example to back up your answer.

   _____

  b) Construct a set of data whose median is one of the data values.

   _____

  c) Construct a set of data whose median is not one of the data values.

   _____

Communicating about Graphs

▶ **GOAL: Use data and graphs to support conclusions.**

1. Stefan's family is moving to Newfoundland. Stefan wants to know more about the population of Newfoundland and Labrador. He obtained the data below from a pamphlet.

   a) Create a graph to organize and display the data in the table below.

   b) Most of the data in the table is organized into nine-year intervals. Some of the data, however, is organized into different intervals. Why might the data be organized in this way?

   c) The town Stefan's parents want to move to has a total population of 1720. Use your graph to write a paragraph predicting how many students go to the local junior middle school. (Assume that students' ages range from 5 to 14 years.)

Population Distribution of Newfoundland and Labrador (thousands)	
Age 0–4	24.8
Age 5–14	63.9
Age 15–19	39.5
Age 20–24	33.8
Age 25–44	151.8
Age 45–54	82.9
Age 55–64	53.0
Age 65–74	35.5
Age 75–84	21.3
Age 85 and over	6.3
Total of all ages	512.8

[Data adapted from Statistics Canada.]

Test Yourself

1. Four Grade 8 classes were asked to choose their favourite Disney Classic from a list of six movies. The results are listed below.

Disney Classic	Number of students
Snow White	30
Bambi	24
Dumbo	30
The Sword and the Stone	12
Pinocchio	6
Sleeping Beauty	18

a) How many students were surveyed?

_____

b) What percent of students chose *Dumbo* as their favourite Disney Classic?

c) Construct a graph to organize and display the data in the table.

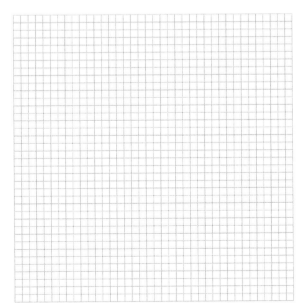

d) How does your graph help you to see at a glance the three most popular Disney Classics?

_____

_____

_____

2. Rishi's class carried out a survey of every student in the school last month. According to the survey, 5% of the students at the school have red hair, 15% have black hair, 60% have brown hair, and 20% have blond hair.

a) Did Rishi's class gather data by taking a census or using a sample? Explain your answer.

_____

_____

b) In Rishi's class of 30 students, 16 students have brown hair, and 3 students have red hair. Calculate the percent of students in Rishi's class with these two colours of hair.

c) Do the percents in Rishi's class agree with the percents in the school population? Why or why not?

_____

_____

_____

3. Construct a comparative bar graph that compares the average heights of plants grown in sunlight with the average heights of plants grown in artificial light.

Average Heights of Plants Grown in Two Types of Light

Day	Plants grown in sunlight (cm)	Plants grown in artificial light (cm)
1	2.1	2.2
2	4.3	3.7
3	6.6	5.3
4	9.0	6.6
5	11.2	8.2
6	14.5	9.6
7	16.8	11.4

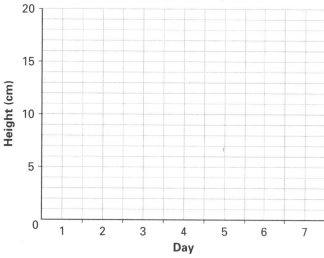

Average Heights of Plants Grown in Two Types of Light

4. Rowyn helps to coach the track-and-field running team. She recorded the following times in seconds for a 50-m practice race.

```
6.5   7.0   9.2   10.4   9.5   8.1
8.8   8.3   6.7   7.0    7.3   8.2
6.4   8.6   7.1   7.8    7.5   9.6
7.7  10.5   7.1   6.9    7.7   6.1
10.2  6.8   8.4   9.7    7.5   7.9
```

a) Organize the data using the frequency table in the next column.

b) Construct a histogram to display the data.

Interval (s)	Frequency
6.0 – 6.9	
7.0 – 7.9	
8.0 – 8.9	
9.0 – 9.9	
10.0 – 10.9	

Running Times for 50-m Race

Frequency

Intervals (s)

c) What are the mean and median of the students who completed the race in 7.0 to 7.9 s?

Mean: _____

Median: _____

d) Rowyn wants 50% of the team to have a time of 7.9 s or less for a 50-m race. Describe how your histogram shows whether the team has achieved this goal or not.

_____

_____

_____

_____

_____

_____

4.1 Exploring Relationships in the Fibonacci Sequence

▶ **GOAL: Identify and discuss relationships within a number pattern.**

1. The Fibonacci sequence is a number pattern that goes like this:

   1, 1, 2, 3, 5, 8, 13, 21, 34, ...

   Starting from the third number, each term in this sequence is the sum of the two preceding terms. Write the next six terms in the Fibonacci sequence.

   > **At-Home Help**
   >
   > A **term** is one number in a sequence. For example, in the sequence 1, 3, 5, 7, ..., the third term is 5.

2. 5, 8, 13, and 21 are four consecutive numbers in the Fibonacci sequence.

   a) Multiply the greatest and the least of these four numbers. _____

   b) Multiply the two middle numbers. _____

   c) By how much do your answers to (a) and (b) differ? _____

3. Repeat the steps in question 2 for other consecutive Fibonacci numbers. What pattern do you notice?

4. **a)** Write any four consecutive Fibonacci numbers. _____

   b) Divide the largest number by the smallest number, and round to one decimal place.

   c) Repeat part (b) three more times using different sets of consecutive Fibonacci numbers. What pattern do you notice?

5. There are many patterns among Fibonacci numbers. Find and describe another pattern when multiplying or dividing Fibonacci numbers.

   _____

   _____

4.2 Creating Pattern Rules from Models

▶ **GOAL: Use algebraic expressions to describe patterns.**

1. For each figure, shade the part of the pattern that stays the same.

At-Home Help

A **variable** is a letter or symbol, such as *a*, *b*, or *n*, that represents a number.

An **algebraic expression** is a combination of one or more variables. It may include numbers and operation symbols.

a)

Figure 1   Figure 2   Figure 3

b)

Figure 1   Figure 2   Figure 3

c)

Figure 1   Figure 2   Figure 3

d)

Figure 1   Figure 2   Figure 3

e)

Figure 1   Figure 2   Figure 3

f)

Figure 1   Figure 2   Figure 3

2. For each part of question 1, draw the next figure in the pattern.

a)

b)

c)

d)

e)

f)

3. For each part of question 1, use an algebraic expression to describe the number of tiles in terms of the figure number.

a) _____

b) _____

c) _____

d) _____

e) _____

f) _____

4. Write an algebraic expression for each pattern. Check your expression by using it to calculate the total number of items in Figure 3.

a) Algebraic expression: _____

Number of tiles in Figure 3: _____

Figure 1   Figure 2   Figure 3

b) Algebraic expression: _____

Number of tiles in Figure 3: _____

Figure 1   Figure 2   Figure 3

c) Algebraic expression: _____

Number of toothpicks in Figure 3: _____

Figure 1   Figure 2   Figure 3

d) Algebraic expression: _____

Number of tiles in Figure 3: _____

Figure 1   Figure 2   Figure 3

5. Use the following description to draw a diagram and write an algebraic pattern rule: "In the first figure, there is one tile on the left, and three tiles stacked in a column on the right. Another column of three tiles is added to each consecutive figure."

Algebraic expression: _____

4.3 The General Term of a Sequence

▶ **GOAL: Write an algebraic expression for the general term of a sequence.**

1. Calculate the 10th term in each sequence.

   a) $n + 3$

   b) $2n + 1$

   c) $3n + 7$

   d) $10n + 5$

2. a) Draw the next two figures in this sequence.

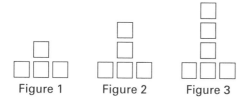

   Figure 1   Figure 2   Figure 3

   b) Fill out the table of values below for the sequence.

Term number (figure number)	1	2	3	4	5
Term value (number of tiles)					

   c) Write an algebraic expression for the *n*th term of the sequence.

   _____

   d) Use your expression for the *n*th term to calculate the 50th term (that is, the 50th figure) in the sequence.

3. Tran is building a sequence of figures out of blocks. The first three figures have three, five, and seven blocks.

   a) Create an algebraic expression for the *n*th term of the sequence.

   _____

   b) Use your algebraic expression to calculate the number of blocks in each of the following figures in the sequence:

   Figure 5   Figure 10

   Figure 25   Figure 100

4. a) Write an algebraic expression for the *n*th term of this sequence. _____

b) Calculate the number of tiles in the 7th figure in this sequence.

Figure 1   Figure 2   Figure 3

c) Calculate the number of tiles in the 17th figure in this sequence.

d) Calculate the number of tiles in the 70th figure in this sequence.

5. Write an algebraic expression for the *n*th term of each sequence. Then use your expression to calculate the 12th and 30th terms in the sequence.

a) 8, 9, 10, 11, ...   Algebraic expression: _____

12th term   30th term

b) 4, 6, 8, 10, ...   Algebraic expression: _____

12th term   30th term

c) 9, 12, 15, 18, ...   Algebraic expression: _____

12th term   30th term

d) 6, 11, 16, 21, ...   Algebraic expression: _____

12th term   30th term

Solve Problems by Examining Simpler Problems

▶ **GOAL:** Solve problems by examining simpler problems first.

1. Before solving each problem, examine a simpler problem first.

   a) Ludek has 22 coins in his pocket. The coins have a total value of $1.45. If the coins are nickels and dimes only, how many of each coin does Ludek have?

   Simpler problem: _____

   _____

   b) There are 20 people in Susan's class. Each person gives a card to everyone else in the class. How many cards were exchanged?

   Simpler problem: _____

   _____

   c) The students at Sunnyside School built a rectangular pyramid of aluminum cans for a world record. The top layer had 2 rows with 3 cans in each row. The second layer had 4 rows of 6 cans. The third layer had 8 rows of 12 cans. How many cans were in the eighth layer of the pyramid?

   Simpler problem: _____

   _____

Relating Number Sequences to Graphs

▶ **GOAL: Relate a sequence to its scatter plot.**

1. Circle the pattern that matches the scatter plot.

   Pattern A: $2n + 5$
   Pattern B: $3n + 4$
   Pattern C: $4n + 3$

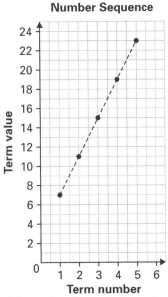

Number Sequence

2. **a)** Use the data in the two tables of values below to draw two scatter plots on the same pair of axes. Use a different colour for each scatter plot.

   Data for Pattern A:

Term number	2	4	6	8
Term value	8	16	24	32

   Data for Pattern B:

Term number	3	6	9	12
Term value	10	16	22	28

   b) Write each pattern rule as an algebraic expression.

   Pattern A: _____   Pattern B: _____

   c) For each scatter plot, determine the term value if the term number is 7.

   d) For each scatter plot, determine the term number if the term value is 20.

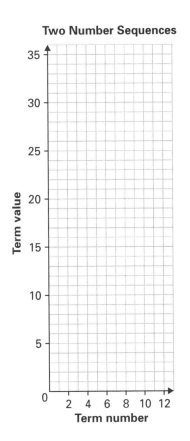

Two Number Sequences

Test Yourself

1. **a)** Which part of this pattern changes?

   _____

   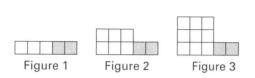

   Figure 1   Figure 2   Figure 3

   b) Use an algebraic expression to describe the number of tiles in terms of the figure number.

   _____

2. Shade the part of each pattern that stays the same. Then write an algebraic expression for each pattern.

   a)

   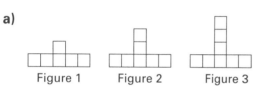

   Figure 1   Figure 2   Figure 3

   Algebraic expression:

   _____

   b)

   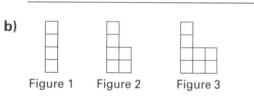

   Figure 1   Figure 2   Figure 3

   Algebraic expression:

   _____

   c)

   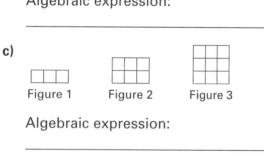

   Figure 1   Figure 2   Figure 3

   Algebraic expression:

   _____

   d)

   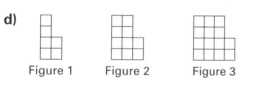

   Figure 1   Figure 2   Figure 3

   Algebraic expression:

   _____

3. Use each description to draw a diagram and write an algebraic pattern rule.

   a) In the first figure, there is one counter on the left, and a column of six counters on the right. Another column of six counters is added to each consecutive figure.

   b) In the first figure, there are nine counters arranged in a square, and two counters sitting on top. For each consecutive figure, two more counters are added on top.

4. **a)** Calculate the term value of the 15th term for the expression $2n + 5$.

   b) Calculate the term value of the 20th term for the expression $4n + 2$.

   c) Calculate the term value of the 10th term for the expression $6n + 5$.

5. **a)** For the expression $3n + 5$, calculate the term number with a value of 26.

b) For the expression $n + 10$, calculate the term number with a value of 34.

c) For the expression $5n + 8$, calculate the term number with a value of 28.

6. a) Complete the table of values for the sequence below.

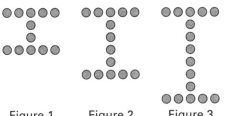

Figure 1   Figure 2   Figure 3

Term number	1	2	3	4	5	6	7	8
Term value	12	14	16					

b) Write an algebraic expression for the nth term of the sequence.

_____

c) Use your algebraic expression to calculate the 50th term in the sequence.

d) What figure number could you make using 32 counters?

7. Write an algebraic expression for the general term of each sequence. Then use your expression to calculate the 30th term in the sequence.

a) 13, 14, 15, 16, …

Algebraic expression:

_____

30th term: _____

b) 10, 12, 14, 16, …

Algebraic expression:

_____

30th term: _____

8. Jordan cuts a large piece of paper in half. Then she cuts each smaller piece of paper in half. If Jordan repeats this pattern 15 times in total, how many pieces of paper will she have?

9. a) Use the data in the table of values to draw a scatter plot.

Term number	1	3	5	7
Term value	9	15	21	27

b) Write an algebraic expression for the pattern. _____

c) Determine the term number if the term value is 4. _____

d) Determine the term value if the term number is 6. _____

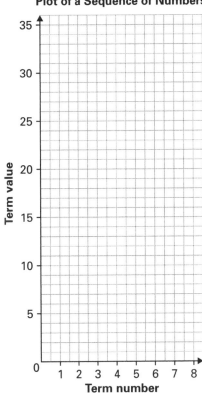

Plot of a Sequence of Numbers

5.1 Exploring Circles

▶ **GOAL: Draw circles and explore measurements.**

1. a) Identify each part of the circle to the right.

A: _____

B: _____

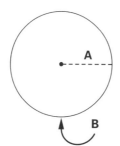

b) Identify each part of the circle to the right.

C: _____

D: _____

E: _____

F: _____

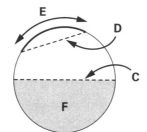

2. What parts of a circle have been used to construct each design?

a)

_____

b)
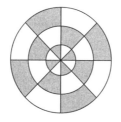
_____

3. Use the circle to construct a design of your own that uses the following:

a) only arcs

b) only chords

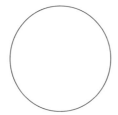

At-Home Help

- The **radius** of a circle is a line segment that goes from the centre of a circle to its circumference. The length of this line segment is also called the radius.

- The **diameter** of a circle is a line segment that runs from one side of the circle, through the centre, to the other side. The length of this line segment is also called the diameter.

- The **circumference** is the boundary of a circle. The length of this boundary is also called the circumference.

- A **semicircle** is one-half of a circle.

- A **chord** is a line segment that joins any two points on the circumference of a circle. The length of this line segment is also called a chord.

- An **arc** is part of the circumference of a circle that lies between two ends of a chord. Each chord creates two arcs. The length of this part is also called an arc.

5.2 Exploring Circumference and Diameter

▶ **GOAL: Investigate the relationship between the diameter and circumference of a circle.**

1. Record the radius and diameter of each circle. To determine the circumference of each circle, measure the amount of string needed to go around the circle.

a) Radius (*r*): _____

Diameter (*d*): _____

Circumference (*C*): _____

$C \div r =$ _____

$C \div d =$ _____

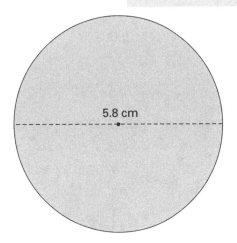

3.2 cm

b) Radius (*r*): _____

Diameter (*d*): _____

Circumference (*C*): _____

$C \div r =$ _____

$C \div d =$ _____

5.8 cm

2. **a)** Find two circular objects in your home. Measure the radius, diameter, and circumference for each circle. Then calculate $C \div r$ and $C \div d$ for each circle.

b) What do you notice about the calculations you performed?

Calculating Circumference

▶ **GOAL: Develop and apply the formula for the circumference of a circle.**

Round your answers to the number of decimal places given.

1. Calculate the circumference of a circle with each diameter.

   a) 4.0 cm
   b) 6.0 cm
   c) 8.0 cm
   d) 10.0 cm

   e) 4.6 cm
   f) 33.7 cm
   g) 72.1 cm
   h) 0.003 cm

At-Home Help

π is the number of times a diameter divides the circumference of a circle. To nine decimal places, the value of π is 3.141 592 654. When you calculate with π, you can use an approximate value such as 3.14.

You can use the formulas below to find the circumference of a circle, where C is the circumference, d is the diameter, and r is the radius of the circle.

$C = \pi d$
or
$C = 2 \pi r$

2. Calculate the circumference of a circle with each radius.

   a) 2.0 cm
   b) 5.0 cm
   c) 20.0 cm

   d) 0.40 cm
   e) 9.2 cm
   f) 12.7 cm

   g) 204.6 cm
   h) 19.36 cm

3. Calculate the diameter of a circle with each circumference.

   a) 22 cm
   b) 60 m

   c) 102.1 mm
   d) 36.7 cm

   e) 178.8 m
   f) 138.94 cm

4. Calculate the radius of a circle with each circumference.

   a) 44 cm
   b) 188 cm

   c) 1.0 cm
   d) 93.6 m

   e) 390.6 mm
   f) 101.1 cm

5. Fill in the blanks.

	Radius	Diameter	Circumference
a)	1.2 cm	2.4 cm	
b)		6.8 cm	
c)			46.5 m
d)	21.5 mm		
e)			31.09 cm

6. An ordinary basketball has a diameter of about 25 cm.
   Calculate the circumference.

7. George Ferris constructed the original Ferris wheel at the midway in Chicago in 1893.

   a) The diameter of the Ferris wheel was 76 m.
      Calculate the circumference.

   b) A small Ferris wheel at a fun fair has a diameter of 14.5 m. One ride consists of three complete turns of the wheel. How far would you travel in one ride?

8. Ken doesn't eat the crust on his pizza. For each pizza, estimate the length of pizza he doesn't eat. Then calculate the length.

   a) radius = 32 cm    b) radius = 12.7 cm

9. The diameter of Sheree's bicycle wheel is 0.705 m. Calculate how many turns the bicycle wheel will make if she rides the bicycle 1 km.

10. A patio umbrella has a diameter of 2.5 m.

    a) Calculate the length of fringe needed for the edge of the umbrella.

    b) What is the cost of the fringe at $6.79/m? Check whether your answer is reasonable.

5.4 Estimating Area

▶ **GOAL: Estimate the area of a circle.**

1. Information on the diameter, circumference, and area of various circles was collected and recorded in the following table. Use a calculator to fill in the missing entries to complete all columns. Record decimals to two places or less.

At-Home Help

You discovered earlier that the circumference of a circle is related to its diameter. The area of a circle is also related to a part of the circle: its radius.

Diameter d	Circumference C	Radius r	Area A	(Radius)^2 r^2	$A \div r^2$
6 cm	18.84 cm		28.26 cm^2		
	37.68 cm		113.04 cm^2		
18 cm			254.34 cm^2		
	75.36 cm		452.16 cm^2		
	94.2 cm		706.5 cm^2		
36 cm			1017.36 cm^2		
	131.88 cm		1384.74 cm^2		
48 cm			1808.64 cm^2		
54 cm			2289.06 cm^2		
	188.4 cm		2826 cm^2		

Conclusion: If $\pi = 3.14$, then $A \div r^2 =$ _____, or $A =$ _____ $\times r^2$

2. You need to buy a cover for your circular pool. If your pool has a radius of 2 m, about how large should the cover be?

   6.5 m^2 9.5 m^2 12.5 m^2 15.5 m^2

3. Reilly is buying glass for a circular table with a 2 m diameter. The hardware store charges $45/m^2 for glass.

   How much will Reilly's glass cost?

5.5 Calculating Area

▶ **GOAL: Develop and apply the formula for the area of a circle.**

1. Estimate the area of each circle. Then calculate.

   At-Home Help

   The formula for the area *A* of a circle with radius *r* is
   $A = \pi r^2$.

   a) radius 10 cm

   Estimation: _____

   Calculation: _____

   b) diameter 4 cm

   Estimation: _____   Calculation: _____

   c) diameter 12 cm

   Estimation: _____   Calculation: _____

   d) radius 4.2 cm

   Estimation: _____   Calculation: _____

   e) radius 101.7 cm

   Estimation: _____   Calculation: _____

   f) diameter 24.3 cm

   Estimation: _____   Calculation: _____

2. An umbrella has a radius of 1.3 m. Calculate the area.

3. An aircraft patrols the sky in a circular area. The area of observation has a radius of 14.5 km. Calculate the area.

4. Calculate the area of the shaded part of each figure.

   a)
   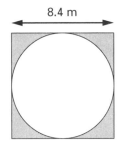

   b)
   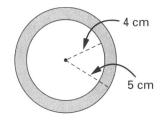

5.6 Solve Problems by Working Backward

▶ **GOAL: Work backward to solve problems.**

Work backward to solve the problems.

1. Calculate the radius of the circle with each measurement.

   a) diameter 6.8 cm

   b) circumference 57.1 m

   c) area 95.0 cm^2

2. Use a compass to draw a circle with an area of 8.8 cm^2. Show your calculations.

3. Miguel and his friends have been hired to paint the fence around a park. Each day they paint twice as much as they did the day before. On the fifth day, they painted 96 m^2.

   a) How much did they paint on the first day?

   b) Miguel and his friends are paid \$4/m^2. How much money did they earn if the fence was finished at the end of the fifth day?

4. The park near Selena's house has a sculpture that looks like a large flat circle standing on its rim. The sculpture's plaque says that it was made from 9.0 m^2 of sheet iron. How tall is the sculpture?

Test Yourself

1. Identify each part of a circle.

   A: _____

   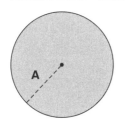

   B: _____

   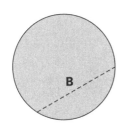

Record your answers to the number of decimals given.

2. Calculate the circumference of a circle with each diameter.

   a) 12 cm   e) 11.7 cm

   b) 2 cm   f) 18.4 cm

   c) 0.5 cm   g) 125.25 cm

   d) 6.8 cm   h) 0.032 cm

3. Calculate the circumference of a circle with each radius.

   a) 7 cm   d) 3.3 cm

   b) 13 cm   e) 16.4 cm

   c) 1.5 cm   f) 88.91 cm

4. A wedge-shaped piece of apple pie is 8.2 cm long from the crust to the tip. What was the circumference of the entire pie?

5. A circular swimming pool has a circumference of 40.8 m. What is the farthest distance you can swim from one side of the pool to the other side?

6. Jordan jogged four times around a circular track with a radius of 8 m. How far did she jog?

7. Calculate the area of a circle with each radius.

   a) 3 cm   e) 1.7 cm

   b) 17 cm   f) 13.9 cm

   c) 0.4 cm   g) 33.58 cm

   d) 0.020 cm   h) 0.00412 cm

8. Calculate the area of a circle with each diameter.

a) 8 cm

e) 1.15 cm

b) 28 cm

f) 9.04 cm

c) 15.1 cm

g) 1000 cm

d) 0.16 cm

h) 0.00303 cm

9. A circular table has a diameter of 1.3 m. What is its area?

10. A face-off circle has a radius of 4.6 m. What is its area?

11. Calculate.

a) the radius of a circle with area 113 m²

b) the diameter of a circle with area 1256 cm²

12. Calculate the area of the shaded region.

a)

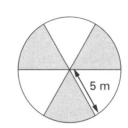

b)

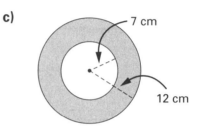

c)

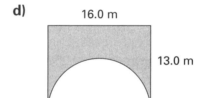

d)

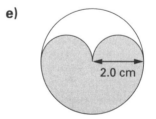

e)

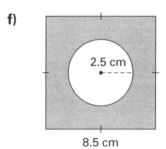

f)

6.1 Exploring Integer Addition and Subtraction

▶ **GOAL: Add and subtract integers.**

1. Write > or < to make each number sentence true.

   a) (-5) _____ $(+5)$

   b) $(+3)$ _____ (-4)

   c) (-8) _____ (-5)

   d) $(+6)$ _____ (-2)

   e) (-11) _____ $(+3)$

   f) (-3) _____ 0

2. Write an integer addition equation for each situation. Then solve your equation, using the number line below. The first one is done for you.

   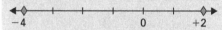
   $-15\ -10\ -5\quad 0\quad +5\ +10\ +15\ +20\ +25$

   a) The temperature this afternoon was $-2°C$. In the evening, the temperature dropped by $3°C$. What was the new temperature?

      $\underline{(-2) + (-3) = (-5)}$

   b) Nathan placed a beaker of ice water, at $0°C$, on a hot plate. The temperature rose by $4°C$. What was the new temperature?

      _____

   c) Yesterday's temperature was $5°C$. Today's temperature is $8°C$ colder. What is today's temperature? _____

3. Write an integer subtraction equation for each situation. Then solve your equation, using the number line below to help you.

   $-25\ -20\ -15\ -10\ -5\quad 0\quad +5\ +10\ +15\ +20\ +25\ +30\ +35$

   a) The highest temperature this summer was $33°C$. The lowest temperature was $18°C$. What is the difference between the two temperatures? _____

   b) The highest temperature last winter was $+3°C$. The lowest temperature was $-23°C$. What is the difference between the two temperatures? _____

At-Home Help

When working with integers, it helps to think of each integer according to its position on a number line. For example, the number line below shows the integers (-4) and $(+2)$. Because $(+2)$ is to the right on the number line, $(+2) > (-4)$.

$-4 \qquad 0 \quad +2$

Here are some rules to help you add and subtract integers using a number line.

- To add a positive integer to any integer, move the same number of spaces to the right on the number line. For example, to find $(-4) + (+2)$, start at (-4) and move two spaces to the right. The answer is (-2).

- To subtract a positive integer, move to the left. For example, $(-4) - (+2) = (-6)$.

- To add a negative integer, move to the left. For example, $(+2) + (-4) = (-2)$.

- To subtract a negative integer, move to the right. For example, $(+2) - (-4) = (+6)$.

Relating Integer Subtraction to Addition

▶ **GOAL: Subtract integers by measuring the distance between them.**

1. **a)** Nathan was asked to calculate $(-15) - 1$. He wrote the equivalent addition statement as $15 + 1$. Was he correct? _____

   b) Selena was asked to calculate $2 - 4$. She rewrote the question as $2 + (-4)$. Was she correct? _____

   c) Annika and Denis were asked to calculate $4 - (-4)$. Annika said this difference was equivalent to $4 + 4$. Denis said it was equivalent to $4 + (-4)$. Who is correct? _____

At-Home Help

Any integer subtraction statement can be rewritten as an equivalent addition statement. Sometimes the addition statement is easier to solve. For example:

$$3 - (-3) = 3 + 3$$
$$= 6$$
$$(-1) - 4 = (-1) + (-4)$$
$$= (-5)$$
$$0 - 4 = 0 + (-4)$$
$$= (-4)$$

2. Write the equivalent addition statement for each difference. Then calculate.

   a) $7 - (-2) =$ _____ = _____

   b) $(-3) - 5 =$ _____ = _____

   c) $0 - 5 =$ _____ = _____

   d) $1 - 3 =$ _____ = _____

   e) $10 - (-11) =$ _____ = _____

   f) $(-4) - 3 =$ _____ = _____

   g) $(-2) - (-4) =$ _____ = _____

   h) $7 - 10 =$ _____ = _____

3. Calculate.

   a) $0 - 9 =$ _____

   b) $(-1) - 3 =$ _____

   c) $7 - (-3) =$ _____

   d) $4 - (-7) =$ _____

   e) $(-3) - 6 =$ _____

   f) $(-9) - (-4) =$ _____

   g) $(-6) - (-7) =$ _____

   h) $13 - 13 =$ _____

   i) $4 - 12 =$ _____

   j) $(-16) - (-18) =$ _____

   k) $20 - (-10) =$ _____

   l) $11 - 19 =$ _____

6.3 Exploring Integer Multiplication

▶ **GOAL: Explore models of, and patterns for, integer multiplication.**

1. a) Jordan calculated the following pattern. Fill in the blanks.

$3 \times 3 = 9$ $3 \times (-1) = (-3)$

$3 \times 2 = \underline{\hspace{1cm}}$ $3 \times 0 = \underline{\hspace{1cm}}$ $3 \times (-2) = (-6)$

$3 \times 1 = 3$ $3 \times (-3) = \underline{\hspace{1cm}}$

b) Based on her pattern, Jordan concluded: "When I multiply two positive integers, the answer is a positive integer." Use Jordan's conclusion to solve each question.

$4 \times 9 = \underline{\hspace{1cm}}$ $12 \times 2 = \underline{\hspace{1cm}}$ $3 \times 11 = \underline{\hspace{1cm}}$

c) Jordan also concluded: "When I multiply a positive integer by a negative integer, the answer is a negative integer." Use Jordan's conclusion to solve each question.

$6 \times (-5) = \underline{\hspace{1cm}}$ $10 \times (-6) = \underline{\hspace{1cm}}$ $5 \times (-4) = \underline{\hspace{1cm}}$

> ### At-Home Help
> When multiplying integers, try multiplying the numbers first. Then figure out what sign the answer will be. For example:
>
> $4 \times (-3)$
>
> The numerical answer will be 12, since $4 \times 3 = 12$.
>
> The sign will be negative, since a positive integer multiplied by a negative integer gives a negative answer. Also, $(-3) + (-3) + (-3) + (-3) = (-12)$.
>
> The answer is (-12).

2. a) Nathan calculated the following pattern. Fill in the missing calculations.

$(-4) \times 3 = (-12)$ $(-4) \times (-1) = 4$

$(-4) \times 2 = (-8)$ $(-4) \times 0 = 0$ $(-4) \times (-2) = \underline{\hspace{1cm}}$

$(-4) \times 1 = \underline{\hspace{1cm}}$ $(-4) \times (-3) = 12$

b) Based on his pattern, Nathan concluded: "When I multiply a negative integer by a positive integer, the answer is a negative integer." Use Nathan's conclusion to solve each question.

$(-3) \times 4 = \underline{\hspace{1cm}}$ $(-1) \times 12 = \underline{\hspace{1cm}}$ $(-7) \times 6 = \underline{\hspace{1cm}}$

c) Nathan also concluded: "When I multiply two negative integers, the answer is a positive integer." Use Nathan's conclusion to solve each question.

$(-5) \times (-5) = \underline{\hspace{1cm}}$ $(-9) \times (-2) = \underline{\hspace{1cm}}$ $(-3) \times (-8) = \underline{\hspace{1cm}}$

3. Complete each statement.

a) positive integer $\times$ positive integer = \underline{\hspace{5cm}}

b) negative integer $\times$ positive integer = \underline{\hspace{5cm}}

c) negative integer $\times$ negative integer = \underline{\hspace{5cm}}

d) positive integer $\times$ negative integer = \underline{\hspace{5cm}}

6.4 Multiplying Integers

▶ **GOAL: Develop and apply strategies to multiply integers.**

1. Teo is using black (negative) and white (positive) counters to model $(-2) \times (-4)$. He reasons, "I can model $2 \times (-4)$ by adding two groups of four negative counters to 0. So I can model $(-2) \times (-4)$ by subtracting two groups of four negative counters from 0."

$$0 - (\bullet\bullet\bullet\bullet\ \bullet\bullet\bullet\bullet)$$

"Next, I will use the zero principle to add eight negative counters and eight positive counters."

What should Teo do next? Complete Teo's explanation and solve.

_____

_____

_____

At-Home Help

When multiplying integers, follow these rules to determine the sign of the answer:
- positive integer × positive integer = positive integer
- positive integer × negative integer = negative integer
- negative integer × positive integer = negative integer
- negative integer × negative integer = positive integer

2. Model using counters, and multiply.

a) $3 \times (-5)$

c) $(-2) \times (-7)$

b) $(-1) \times (-6)$

d) $5 \times (-2)$

Copyright © 2006 by Nelson Education Ltd.

3. Tamara is using a number line to model $(-3) \times (-3)$. She reasons, "$(-3) \times (-3)$ means the opposite of $3 \times (-3)$. To show $3 \times (-3)$, I can draw three dotted arrows going left from 0, with each arrow 3 units. The arrows stop at -9."

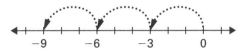

"To show the opposite of $3 \times (-3)$, I can draw three solid arrows going right from -9 back to 0."

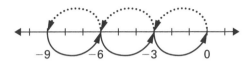

What should Tamara do next? Complete Tamara's explanation and solve.

_____

_____

_____

4. Model using number lines, and multiply.

a) $5 \times (-1)$ **c)** $7 \times (-3)$

b) $(-4) \times (-4)$ **d)** $(-6) \times (-4)$

5. Multiply.

a) $8 \times 9 =$ _____   **e)** $-5(-15) =$ _____

b) $(-8) \times (-8) =$ _____   **f)** $5(-12) =$ _____

c) $-4(2) =$ _____   **g)** $-8(-20) =$ _____

d) $-10(-7) =$ _____   **h)** $17(-4) =$ _____

6. Write an integer multiplication sentence for each description, then solve.

a) The water temperature dropped 5°C per minute, for 13 minutes.

_____

b) The temperature soared 8°C per day, for three days.

_____

Exploring Integer Division

▶ **GOAL: Explore models and patterns for integer division.**

1. Teo wanted to model $(-10) \div 5$ using counters. He started with 10 black counters, each representing -1.

What should Teo do next? Use pictures and words to complete Teo's explanation and find the answer.

2. Selena wanted to model $(-14) \div 7$ using a number line. She drew an arrow from 0 to -14 on a number line.

What should Selena do next? Use pictures and words to complete Selena's explanation and find the answer.

3. a) Annika calculated the following pattern. Fill in the missing calculations.

$10 \div 2 = $ _____ $(-2) \div 2 = $ _____

$6 \div 2 = 3$ $(-6) \div 2 = (-3)$

$2 \div 2 = 1$ $(-10) \div 2 = (-5)$

b) Based on her pattern, Annika concluded: "When I divide two positive integers, the answer is a positive integer." Use Annika's conclusion to solve each question.

$28 \div 4 = $ _____ $15 \div 5 = $ _____ $81 \div 9 = $ _____

c) Annika also concluded: "When I divide a negative integer by a positive integer, the answer is a negative integer." Use Annika's conclusion to solve each question, and then check by multiplying.

$(-20) \div 4 = $ _____ or $4 \times $ _____ $= (-20)$

$(-35) \div 5 = $ _____ or $5 \times $ _____ $= (-35)$

$(-27) \div 9 = $ _____ or $9 \times $ _____ $= (-27)$

4. a) Denis calculated the following pattern. Fill in the missing calculations.

$12 \div (-4) = $ _____

$8 \div (-4) = -2$ $0 \div (-4) = 0$

$4 \div (-4) = $ _____

$(-4) \div (-4) = 1$

$(-8) \div (-4) = $ _____

$(-12) \div (-4) = 3$

b) Based on his pattern, Denis concluded: "When I divide a positive integer by a negative integer, the answer is a negative integer." Use Denis's conclusion to solve each question, and then check by multiplying.

$48 \div (-6) = $ _____ or $(-6) \times $ _____ $= 48$

$30 \div (-3) = $ _____ or $(-3) \times $ _____ $= 30$

$36 \div (-9) = $ _____ or $(-9) \times $ _____ $= 36$

c) Denis also concluded: "When I divide two negative integers, the answer is a positive integer." Use Denis's conclusion to solve each question, and then check by multiplying.

$(-49) \div (-7) = $ _____ or $(-7) \times $ _____ $= (-49)$

$(-16) \div (-1) = $ _____ or $(-1) \times $ _____ $= (-16)$

$(-50) \div (-10) = $ _____ or $(-10) \times $ _____ $= (-50)$

5. Calculate each pattern.

a) $(-15) \div 5 = $ _____

$(-10) \div 5 = $ _____

$(-5) \div 5 = $ _____

$5 \div 5 = $ _____

$10 \div 5 = $ _____

$15 \div 5 = $ _____

b) $(-30) \div (-6) = $ _____

$(-18) \div (-6) = $ _____

$(-6) \div (-6) = $ _____

$6 \div (-6) = $ _____

$18 \div (-6) = $ _____

$30 \div (-6) = $ _____

6. Complete each statement.

a) positive integer $\div$ positive integer $= $ _____

b) negative integer $\div$ positive integer $= $ _____

c) negative integer $\div$ negative integer $=$ _____

d) positive integer $\div$ negative integer $= $ _____

6.6 Dividing Integers

▶ **GOAL: Develop and apply strategies to divide integers.**

1. Write each multiplication equation as a division equation, then solve. The first one is done for you.

   a) $3 \times$ _____ $= (-12)$ Division: $\underline{(-12) \div 3 = (-4)}$

   b) $(-2) \times$ _____ $= (-6)$ Division: _____

   c) $7 \times$ _____ $= 35$ Division: _____

   d) $(-5) \times$ _____ $= (-55)$ Division: _____

   e) $(-8) \times$ _____ $= 8$ Division: _____

   f) $(-4) \times$ _____ $= 0$ Division: _____

At-Home Help

When dividing integers, follow these rules to determine the sign of the answer:

- positive integer ÷ positive integer = positive integer
- positive integer ÷ negative integer = negative integer
- negative integer ÷ positive integer = negative integer
- negative integer ÷ negative integer = positive integer

2. Write a multiplication equation for each division. Then solve the division.

   a) $(-56) \div 7 =$ _____   c) $54 \div -6 =$ _____

   Multiplication: _____   Multiplication: _____

   b) $(-30) \div 3 =$ _____   d) $(-22) \div -2 =$ _____

   Multiplication: _____   Multiplication: _____

3. Divide. Multiply to check.

   a) $(-26) \div (-2) =$ _____   d) $(-100) \div (-2) =$ _____

   b) $17 \div (-1) =$ _____   e) $(-24) \div 8 =$ _____

   c) $44 \div (-11) =$ _____   f) $(-60) \div 15 =$ _____

4. Fill in the missing integer in each equation.

   a) $6 \times$ _____ $= (-12)$ b) $(-10) \times$ _____ $= 30$ c) $(-5) \times$ _____ $= (-40)$

5. Use a calculator to divide.

   a) $(-345) \div 5 =$ _____   d) $(-224) \div 7 =$ _____

   b) $(-120) \div (-15) =$ _____   e) $357 \div (-21) =$ _____

   c) $437 \div (-19) =$ _____   f) $(-990) \div (-45) =$ _____

6.7 Order of Operations with Integers

▶ **GOAL: Apply the rules for the order of operations with integers.**

1. Calculate.

a) $(-36) \div [(-6) \div (-6)]$ **b)** $[(-36) \div (-6)] \div (-6)$

Why are your answers to (a) and (b) different?

_____

_____

2. Calculate.

a) $(-4) + 16 \div (-4)$ **d)** $(-8) \div [(-4) + 2]$

b) $[(-4) + 16] \div (-4)$ **e)** $(-8) - [(-4) \div 2]$

c) $(-8) \div (-4) + 2$ **f)** $[(-8) - (-4)] \div 2$

3. Calculate.

a) $(-3) + (-3) \times (-3)$ **d)** $15 - (-9) \div 3$

b) $12 \div (-4) + (-8)$ **e)** $[(-4) + (-16) - (-5)] \div (-3)$

c) $(-2) \times (-7) - (-8)$ **f)** $(-10) \times (-1) + 6 \times (-4)$

4. Nathan and Selena were given the expression $8 \times (-2) - (-5) \times 4$ to calculate. Each student got a different answer.

Nathan's Solution

$$8 \times (-2) - (-5) \times 4 = (-16) - (-5) \times 4$$
$$= (-11) \times 4$$
$$= (-44)$$

Selena's Solution

$$8 \times (-2) - (-5) \times 4 = 8 \times 3 \times 4$$
$$= 96$$

a) What error did Nathan make?

_____

b) What error did Selena make?

_____

c) Solve the expression.

5. Calculate.

a) $[(-5 + 7)] \times (-3)$

d) $(-20) \div 2 - (-5) \times (-3)$

b) $11 + (-5) \times 5$

e) $[(-1) \times (-2) - (9)] \times (-3)$

c) $(-6) \div [(-8) + 2]$

f) $(-10) \times (-4) + (-8) - 20$

6. Place brackets in each expression to get the appropriate answer.

a) $(-8) - 12 \div (-4) = 5$

b) $5 - (-5) \times (-4) + 2 = -20$

7. Calculate.

a) $\dfrac{(-12) + (-4)}{(-15) + 11}$

c) $\dfrac{(-6) + (-2) - (-1)}{5 + (-4)}$

b) $\dfrac{7 - 12 + (-3)}{(-3) \times 6 \div (-9)}$

d) $\dfrac{5 \times (-4) - (-10)}{(-8) + 16 - (-2)}$

8. Mineral deposits are found at the following depths: -232 m, -321 m, -225 m, -154 m. Find the average of the depths.

Communicating about Calculations

▶ **GOAL: Explain your thinking when solving integer problems.**

Use the Communication Checklist to help you explain your answer to each question.

1. Teo started with $560 in his bank account. During the week, he spent $55 on a pair of shoes, and $123 on a new suit. Then he deposited a cheque for $264. Finally, Teo loaned his sister $45.

   Write an integer to represent the value of Teo's bank account at the end of the week. Explain your thinking.

   _____

   _____

   _____

2. Today's temperature was −2°C. Yesterday, the temperature rose 4°C. Two days ago, the temperature dropped 10°C. What was the original temperature two days ago? Explain your thinking.

   _____

   _____

3. On a shopping trip, Jordan started in the centre of the mall. She walked 25 m west to Jeans & Things, and then 16 m east to Paradise Shoes. Next, she walked 38 m west to Sara's Dresses. Finally, she walked 19 m east to The Vanity Shop.

   Use an integer to describe Jordan's final position. Explain your thinking.

   _____

   _____

   _____

Test Yourself

1. Write an equivalent addition expression for each subtraction. Then calculate. The first one is done for you.

   a) $5 - 7 =$ _____$5 + (-7)$_____ $=$ __-2__

   b) $(-2) - 1 =$ _____ $=$ _____

   c) $9 - 7 =$ _____ $=$ _____

   d) $11 - 20 =$ _____ $=$ _____

   e) $(-4) - (-2) =$ _____ $=$ _____

   f) $7 - (-3) =$ _____ $=$ _____

2. Calculate.

   a) $12 - 7 =$ _____

   b) $8 - 15 =$ _____

   c) $(-10) - 4 =$ _____

   d) $(-7) - 15 =$ _____

   e) $9 - (-3) =$ _____

   f) $(-3) - (-5) =$ _____

   g) $(-9) + 7 =$ _____

   h) $(-12) + 15 =$ _____

3. Write the multiplication sentence that each model represents, and then solve.

   a)
   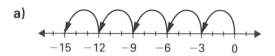
   _____

   b)

   _____

   c)
   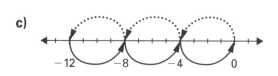
   _____

4. Use counters to model $3 \times (-6)$, and then solve.

5. Write an integer multiplication sentence for each description. Solve your sentence.

   a) Tamara walked west for 3 h at 6 km/h.
   _____

   b) The temperature rose for two days at 5°C/day.
   _____

6. Write the related multiplication equation for each division equation.

   a) $8 \div (-2)$ is equivalent to
   _____

   b) $(-5) \div (-1)$ is equivalent to
   _____

   c) $(-10) \div 2$ is equivalent to
   _____

   d) $18 \div (-6)$ is equivalent to
   _____

7. Calculate.

   a) $(-6) \times 5 =$ _____

   b) $4 \times (-8) =$ _____

   c) $16 \div (-8) =$ _____

   d) $(-24) \div 3 =$ _____

   e) $(-5) \times (-5) =$ _____

   f) $18 \div (-1) =$ _____

g) $(-20) \div (-5) =$ _____

h) $7 \times (-10) =$ _____

i) $30 \div (-6) =$ _____

j) $(-110) \div 2 =$ _____

k) $(-40) \times (-3) =$ _____

l) $15 \times (-4) =$ _____

m) $3 \times (-1) \times (-4) =$ _____

n) $(-8) \div 2 \div (-2) =$ _____

o) $(-5) \times (-4) \div (-10) =$ _____

8. Use a calculator to evaluate.

a) $(-34) \times 234 =$ _____

b) $(-178) \times (-56) =$ _____

c) $828 \div (-18) =$ _____

d) $(-915) \div (-15) =$ _____

9. Calculate.

a) $(-6) \times 3 - 2$

b) $(-4) - 2 \times (-2)$

c) $(-6) + (-12) \div (-2)$

d) $(-6) \times (-3) \div 9$

e) $[(-9) + 1] \div (-4)$

f) $(-3) \times (-7) + 2$

g) $(-15) \div [(-3) -2]$

h) $[(-8) - 3] + 5$

10. Calculate.

a) $(-6) \times (-8) \div 2 + 36$

b) $(-12) + 8 - 6 \div 3 + 2 \times (-3)$

c) $\dfrac{(-8) - 36}{(-11)}$

d) $\dfrac{(-56) + 21}{(-5) \times (-7)}$

11. The temperature on Monday was 10°C. On each of the following three days, the temperature dropped by 2°C. On Friday, the temperature rose 9°C. Write an expression describing the final temperature. Solve your expression.

Coordinates of Points on a Grid

▶ **GOAL: Graph points using the four quadrants of a Cartesian coodinate system.**

1. Name the coordinates for each point.

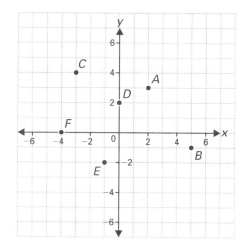

A: _____

B: _____

C: _____

D: _____

E: _____

F: _____

2. Plot these points on the grid below.

A (4, 3)

B (0, −1)

C (2, −5)

D (−3, 3)

E (−5, 0)

F (−2, −2)

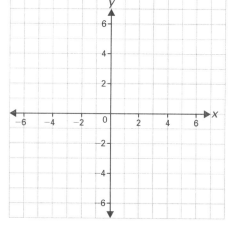

3. Write the words "right" or "left" to make each statement true.

   a) (4, 4) is to the _____ of (3, 3).   **c)** (−1, −1) is to the _____ of (−3, 2).

   b) (−2, 3) is to the _____ of (0, 2).   **d)** (7, −4) is to the _____ of (−8, −5).

4. Write the words "above" or "below" to make each statement true.

   a) (3, 3) is _____ (2, 2).   **c)** (−4, −4) is _____ (−6, 3).

   b) (−5, 1) is _____ (5, 0).   **d)** (2, −9) is _____ (−1, −1).

5. A square has the vertices E (1, 3), F (1, −2), and G (6, −2). What are the missing coordinates of the fourth vertex, H? _____

Translations on a Coordinate System

▶ **GOAL: Graph the results of a translation on a coordinate grid.**

1. For each point, write the new coordinates after the translation.

   a) (3, 5) after [1, 1] _____

   b) (−1, 4) after [−2, −2] _____

   c) (6, −2) after [5, 5] _____

   d) (−4, −8) after [−3, −5] _____

2. **a)** On the grid below, draw the image of rectangle *ABCD* after the translation [4, −2].

   b) Write the coordinates of the image.

   _____

   _____

   _____

   _____

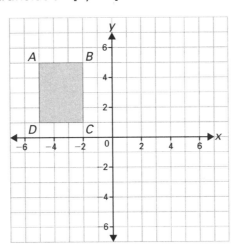

3. A triangle has the vertices *A*(2, 2), *B*(3, 5), and *C*(4, 1). After a translation, the image of the triangle has the vertices *A*′(−1, 3), *B*′(0, 6), and *C*′(1, 2). Calculate and write the translation vector.

4. Write the vector for the translation that moved *EFGH* to *E*′*F*′*G*′*H*′. _____

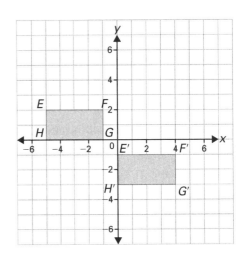

7.3 Reflections and Rotations

▶ **GOAL: Graph the results of reflections and rotations on a coordinate grid.**

1. Determine the new coordinates for each point after it is reflected in the *x*-axis.

    a) (4, 5) → _____   **c)** (−5, −7) → _____

    b) (−3, 2) → _____   **d)** (1, −5) → _____

2. Determine the new coordinates for each point after it is reflected in the *y*-axis.

    a) (2, 2) →_____   **c)** (−8, −3) → _____

    b) (−4, 1) → _____   **d)** (4, −6) → _____

3. On the grid below, draw the image of triangle *ABC* after a 90° cw rotation about the origin.

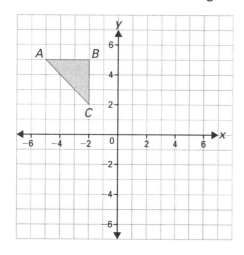

4. On the grid below, draw the image of quadrilateral *DEFG* after a reflection in the *x*-axis.

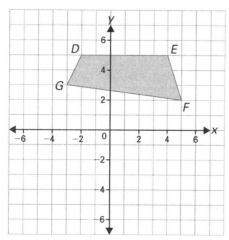

At–Home Help

• A **reflection** is the result of a flip of a 2-D shape; each point in the 2-D shape flips to the opposite side of the line of reflection, but stays the same distance from the line.

• A **rotation** is a transformation in which each point in a shape moves about a fixed point (the centre of rotation) through the same angle.

• The **centre of rotation** is a fixed point around which other points in a shape rotate in a clockwise (cw) or counterclockwise (ccw) direction. The centre of rotation may be inside or outside the shape.

To rotate a shape on a Cartesian grid, follow these steps for each point in the shape:

Step 1: Draw a line from the point to the centre of rotation.

Step 2: Use a protractor to measure the angle of rotation (for example, 90° in a clockwise direction). Draw another line segment at this angle.

Step 3: Place the point of a compass on the centre of rotation, and the pencil on the point. Draw an arc from the point to meet the new line segment. Mark the new image point here.

Step 4: Repeat steps 1 to 3 for each point in the shape.

7.4 Exploring Similar Shapes

▶ **Investigate the properties of similar shapes.**

1. Pairs of similar triangles are shown on the grid below.

a) In triangle *ABC* and triangle *DEF*, one pair of corresponding sides is *AC* and *DF*. Measure the corresponding sides of each pair of triangles.

b) Find the ratios of the measures of the corresponding sides. In triangle *ABC* and triangle *DEF*, the ratios are $\frac{AC}{DF}$, $\frac{AB}{DE}$, and $\frac{BC}{EF}$.

c) What do you notice about the ratios of corresponding sides in similar triangles?

_____

_____

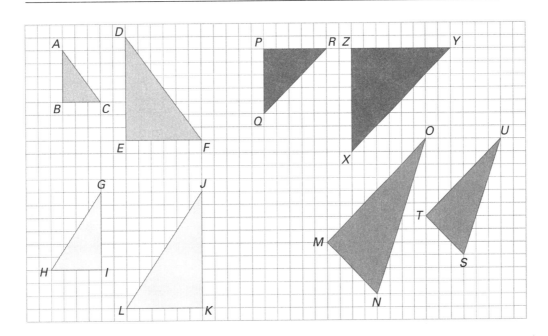

2. Fill in the missing measures for the pair of similar triangles below.

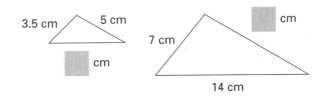

7.5 Communicating about Transformations

▶ **GOAL: Describe transformations of geometric figures.**

1. Use the Communication Checklist to describe each transformation or set of transformations.

a)

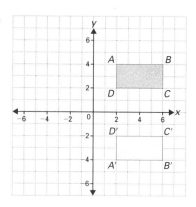

Description: _____

_____

_____

b)

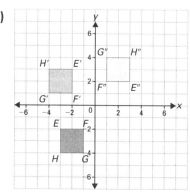

Description: _____

_____

_____

_____

_____

_____

c)

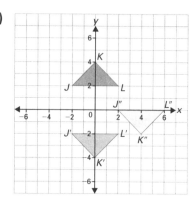

Description: _____

_____

_____

_____

_____

_____

Test Yourself

1. Plot the following coordinates on the grid below.

   $A(1, 3)$

   $B(3, -4)$

   $C(-4, -2)$

   $D(0, 5)$

   $E(-5, 5)$

   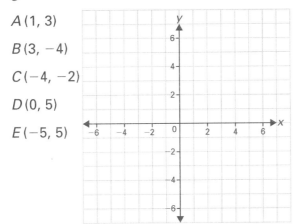

2. Place the following coordinates in order, from the point farthest left to the point farthest right.

   _____

   $A(3, 3)$ $C(0, -2)$ $E(30, 5)$

   $B(-7, -4)$ $D(-1, 5)$ $F(-12, -14)$

3. Place the following coordinates in order, from the point farthest down to the point farthest up.

   _____

   $A(2, 4)$ $C(0, -2)$ $E(11, 17)$

   $B(-1, -16)$ $D(-1, 0)$ $F(-3, 5)$

4. Write the coordinates of each point after the translation.

   a) $(3, 4)$ after $[1, 1]$ _____

   b) $(-2, 0)$ after $[5, -1]$ _____

   c) $(8, 8)$ after $[-4, -4]$ _____

   d) $(3, -5)$ after $[-6, 7]$ _____

   e) $(-10, -12)$ after $[13, 13]$ _____

   f) $(16, -3)$ after $[-9, 11]$ _____

5. A triangle with the vertices $A(4, 4)$, $B(6, 1)$, and $C(2, 2)$ is translated $[-4, 2]$. What are the vertex coordinates of the image?

6. After a translation of $[0, -3]$, an image has the vertex coordinates $E'(-4, -6)$, $F'(-3, -2)$, $G'(-1, -5)$, and $H'(1, 0)$. What were the vertex coordinates of the original image?

7. a) Plot the points $A(-3, 1)$, $B(-1, 4)$, $C(5, 4)$, $D(3, 1)$ on the grid below, and join the dots to form a polygon.

   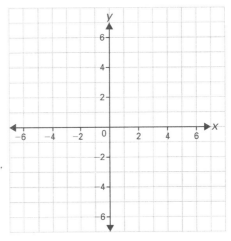

   b) Name the shape of the polygon.

   _____

c) Reflect polygon *ABCD* in the *x*-axis. Write the coordinates of the image.

_____

_____

d) Reflect polygon *ABCD* in the *y*-axis. Write the coordinates of the image.

_____

_____

e) Rotate polygon *ABCD* 180° clockwise around the origin. Write the coordinates of the image.

_____

_____

8. a) Draw the image of quadrilateral *EFGH* after a reflection in the *y*-axis.

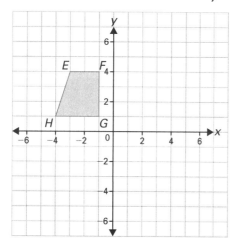

b) Draw the image of triangle *JKL* after a 90° counterclockwise rotation around the origin.

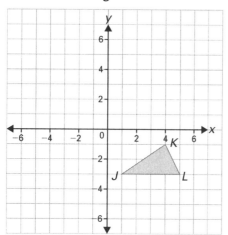

c) Draw the image of triangle *MNO* after a translation of [−6, −4].

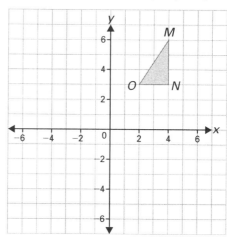

9. Fill in the missing measures for the pair of similar triangles below.

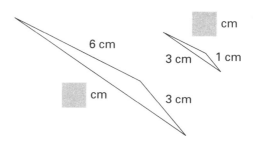

10. Triangle 1 and triangle 2 are similar. Each side of triangle 1 is twice as long as the corresponding side of triangle 2.

a) The angles of triangle 1 are 30°, 70°, and 80°. What are the angles of triangle 2?

_____

b) The perimeter of triangle 1 is 20 cm. What is the perimeter of triangle 2?

_____

11. Write a description of how you would transform the top left triangle to create the pattern on the grid to the right.

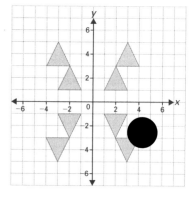

_____

_____

8.1 Solving Equations by Graphing

▶ **GOAL: Use tables and graphs to solve equations.**

1. To solve the equation $6n - 5 = 37$, Rishi decided to construct a table of values, and then plot a graph.

   a) Complete Rishi's table of values for the equation.

Term number (n)	1	2	3	4	5
Term value ($6n - 5$)	1	7			

   b) Using the table of values, draw a graph on the grid. Extend the line of your graph, and then use your graph to find the solution to the equation.

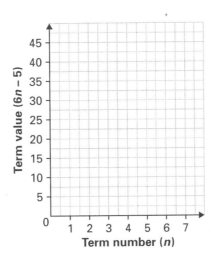

2. a) Fill out the table of values for the pattern below.

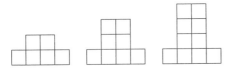

Term number	1	2	3	4	5
Term value	6	8			

   b) Write an algebraic expression for the pattern rule. _____

   c) Create an equation to determine the figure number of the figure with 24 squares.

   _____

   d) Draw a graph on the grid to solve your equation in part (c).

   e) Check your solution by substituting it for the variable in the equation.

▶ GOAL: Represent a pattern relationship using a chart, an equation, and a graph.

1. Rowyn is making cookies for the school fair. On the first day, she made 4 trays of cookies. On the second day, she made 6 trays of cookies. On each day after that, she made 2 trays more than she did the day before.

a) Draw a series of figures to model the problem.

b) Write an equation for the pattern. Use your equation to calculate the day on which Rowyn made 14 trays of cookies.

At-Home Help

When working with pattern relationships, try looking at each problem in more than one way. The following methods can help you solve a pattern problem:

- Use counters or toothpicks to model the problem.
- Write an equation for the problem, and then solve to find the value of the variable.
- Prepare a chart to organize the information, and use it to solve the problem.
- Draw a graph to help you solve the problem.

c) Rowyn wants to make a total of 88 trays of cookies. Fill in the table of values, and then plot the data on a graph. Extend the line on your graph. How many days will it take for Rowyn to achieve her goal?

Day	1	2	3	4	5
Number of trays	4	6	8		
Total number of trays	4	10			

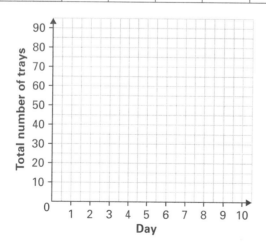

Copyright © 2006 by Nelson Education Ltd.

8.3 Creating and Evaluating Algebraic Expressions

▶ **GOAL: Use algebraic expressions to represent calculations.**

1. Kito earned money this summer by mowing lawns and babysitting. He earned $20 for each lawn he mowed, and $30 for each babysitting job.

   a) Write an algebraic expression for the total income Kito earned this summer.

   _____

   b) Kito mowed 10 lawns and did 5 babysitting jobs in July. Use your expression in part (a) to calculate his total income in July.

   At–Home Help

   An algebraic expression can have more than one variable. For example, the expression $4a + 2b$ has two variables: a and b. If you know the value of both variables, you can find the value of the expression. For example, if $a = 1$ and $b = 2$, then
   $$4a + 2b = 4(1) + 2(2)$$
   $$= 4 + 4$$
   $$= 8$$

2. Rishi is selling juice and popcorn at the school fair. Each can of juice costs $1.25, and each bag of popcorn costs $0.75.

   a) Write an expression for the total amount of money Rishi received from the sales. _____

   b) In the first hour, Rishi sold 8 cans of juice and 12 bags of popcorn. Use your expression in part (a) to calculate the total amount of money he collected.

3. Find the value of each expression.

   a) $2a + 7$, where $a = 3$

   b) $3x - 3$, where $x = 6$

   c) $5m + 2n$, where $m = 1$ and $n = 2$

   d) $2c + 4d$, where $c = 3$ and $d = 3$

   e) $10e - 2f$, where $e = 4$ and $f = 5$

   f) $3r - s + 2$, where $r = 6$ and $s = 1$

Solving Equations I

▶ **GOAL: Solve equations using inspection, systematic trial, and graphing.**

1. Estimate each solution.

   a) $5x = 26$

   b) $2x + 4 = 8.5$

   c) $15x = 146$

   d) $7 - 1.2x = 4$

2. Solve.

   a) $n + 3 = 7$

   b) $1 = 5 - n$

   c) $2n + 3 = 19$

   d) $6 + 3n = 27$

   e) $6 = 3.5 + n$

   f) $5n = 6.5$

   g) $4n + 1.6 = 10.4$

   h) $11.9 = 3.5 + 2n$

3. Estimate each answer. Then use guessing and testing to solve.

   a) $13x + 9 = 61$

   b) $2 + 19p = 125.5$

   c) $14.2w - 2.1 = 97.3$

4. Rowyn was given the equation $12p + 111 = 285$ to solve. Part of her solution is shown below. Complete Rowyn's solution by filling out the table.

   Rowyn's Solution: "First, I estimated the answer. 12 is close to 10, and 111 is close to 100. 285 is close to 250."

   $$10p + 100 = 250$$
   $$10p = 150 \qquad p \text{ is about } 15.$$

   "I used my estimation to start guessing and testing in this table."

Predict p.	Evaluate 12p + 111	Is the answer 285?
15	$12(15) + 111 = 291$	No, it's too high.

5. Write an equation for each situation. Then solve your equation.

   a) A number is multiplied by 20. The result is 200.

   b) A number is multiplied by 3, and then subtracted from 7. The result is 1.

6. Max wants to earn $198 to buy some new sports equipment. He has $78 in his bank account. His mom says she will pay him $15 every time he washes the car.

   a) Draw a graph to show this situation. Put the number of times Max washes the car on the x-axis, and the total amount of money he has on the y-axis.

   b) Use your graph to estimate how many times Max will have to wash the car. _____

   c) Write an equation that relates the number of times Max washes the car to the total amount of money he has.

   _____

   d) Solve your equation. Compare your solution to your answer to part (b).

Solving Equations II

▶ **GOAL: Solve equations by balancing.**

1. a) Look at the diagram below. Suppose that you subtract two counters from the left side. What must you do on the right side to keep the balance? _____

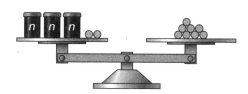

b) Write an equation for the diagram.

_____

c) Solve your equation using a model or another diagram. Show your steps.

2. a) Draw a diagram to model the equation $4x + 3 = 15$.

b) Solve the equation. Draw a diagram for each step of your solution.

At-Home Help

You can solve an equation by balancing. To do this, model the equation using marbles, containers, and a pan balance. For example:

$2x + 5 = 13$

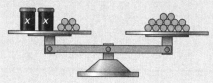

To find the solution, you need to figure out how many marbles are in each container. First, you can take five marbles away from both sides.

$$2x + 5 - 5 = 13 - 5$$
$$2x = 8$$

Next, you can divide both sides of the equation into two sections.

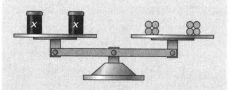

$$2x \div 2 = 8 \div 2$$

Match one of the containers on the left side with one of the groups of marbles on the right side.

$x = 4$

There are four marbles in each container.

3. Solve each equation. Show your steps.

a) $p + 2 = 9$

d) $5w - 3 = 12$

b) $3b + 6 = 15$

e) $5 = 13 - k$

c) $11 = z - 1$

f) $6v = 42$

4. During a magic trick, a magician shows the audience 3 closed bags. Each bag contains an equal number of jewels. The magician's assistant reaches into one bag and takes out 4 jewels. The magician tells the audience that there are now a total of 14 jewels left in the 3 bags.

a) Write an equation for this situation.

_____

b) Solve your equation. How many jewels were in each bag at the beginning of the trick?

5. Hoshi has 6 bags. Each bag contains the same number of marbles. Hoshi also has 8 marbles in his pocket. In total, he has 38 marbles. How many marbles are in each bag?

6. Solve.

a) $2.3 = 1.7 + m$

b) $3.5 + 2x = 17.5$

c) $x \div 5 - 0.5 = 0.8$

8.6 Communicating about Equations

▶ **GOAL: Describe how to create and solve problems.**

1. Rowyn created a problem that is represented by the equation $3k - 2 = 10$.

   Rowyn's Problem: "I bought three bags of granola bars. My little brother ate 2 granola bars. There were 10 granola bars left over. How many granola bars were in each bag?"

   a) Explain how Rowyn's problem matches the equation.

   _____

   _____

   _____

   b) Solve Rowyn's problem.

2. **a)** Create a problem that can be represented by the equation $4b + 1.75 = 10.55$.

   _____

   _____

   _____

   b) Solve your problem.

   c) Explain how you created your problem and how you solved it. Use the Communication Checklist to help you.

   _____

   _____

   _____

   _____

Test Yourself

1. Use the graph below. What is the solution to the equation $3x + 4 = 19$?

   _____

   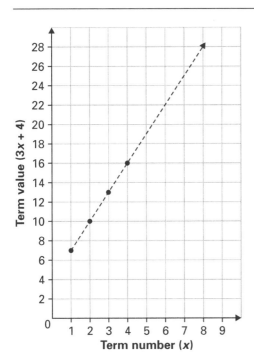

2. A snack bar sells two types of granola bars. An apricot bar costs $0.80, and a cranberry bar costs $1.25.

   a) Write an algebraic expression that represents the income the snack bar makes from selling granola bars.

   _____

   b) Kayley bought four apricot granola bars and two cranberry granola bars. Evaluate your expression to find out how much she spent.

3. a) Complete the table of values below.

Term number (*n*)	1	2	3	4	5
Term value	10	12	14		

b) Write an algebraic expression for the pattern rule.

_____

c) Create an equation to determine the term number if the term value is 22.

_____

d) Draw a graph to solve your equation in part (c).

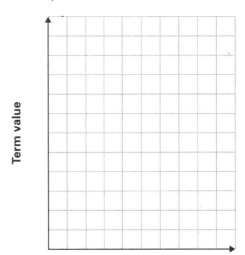

Term number

4. Calculate the value of each expression.

   a) $4a + 2$, where $a = 7$

   b) $6 - 3b$, where $b = 1$

   c) $20 + 10c$, where $c = 3$

   d) $3p - q$, where $p = 9$ and $q = 4.6$

5. Ling is two times Jordan's age, plus three years.

   a) Write an algebraic expression for Ling's age.

   _____

   b) How old is Ling if Jordan is 12?

6. Caitlyn has a sealed bag of fruit bars and cereal squares. The bag contains a mixture of fruit bars and cereal squares. A fruit bar weighs 75 g, and a cereal square weighs 14 g.

   a) Write an algebraic expression for the total mass of f fruit bars and c cereal squares.

   _____

   b) If there are 3 fruit bars and 9 cereal squares, what is the mass of the bag?

7. Solve.

   a) $10 = a + 5$ **c)** $10y + 15 = 115$

   b) $2b - 3 = 11$ **d)** $z + 1.5 = 7.5$

8. Nine coins are used to pay a bill of $1.35. The coins are all quarters and dimes. How many quarters are there? Continue filling out the chart to find the answer.

Quarters	Dimes	Total
1	8	$1.05 (too low)

9. Estimate each solution.

   a) $31 = 6b$ **c)** $4y + 6.2 = 14$

   b) $108 - 10x = 0$ **d)** $19.2 = 8h - 4.9$

10. Write an equation for the diagram. Solve your equation.

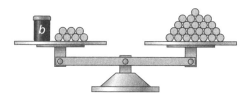

11. Five bags of marbles, plus 3 marbles, equals 33 marbles. Each bag has the same number of marbles.

   a) Draw a diagram to model this situation.

   b) How many marbles are in each bag?

12. Create a problem for the equation $1.7 + 3k = 18.2$. Then solve your problem and explain your solution.

9.1 Adding and Subtracting Fractions Less Than 1

▶ **GOAL: Add and subtract fractions less than 1.**

1. Use the number line below to add $\frac{1}{4} + \frac{1}{5}$.

   0 ├─────────────────────────┤ 1

At-Home Help

When a fraction is renamed as an equivalent fraction with a numerator and a denominator that are lower numbers, we say that the renamed fraction is in lower terms. If there is no way to rename a fraction in even lower terms, we say it is in **lowest terms**, or simplest form. For example, $\frac{12}{24}$ can be written as $\frac{6}{12}$ in lower terms or as $\frac{1}{2}$ in lowest terms.

2. Use the fraction strips below to subtract $\frac{2}{3} - \frac{1}{2}$.

   ▭▭▭ − ▭▭▭ = ▭▭▭

3. Draw counters on the grid below to add $\frac{3}{4} + \frac{1}{6}$. Draw a second grid if you need it. Simplify the answer into lowest terms.

4. Add or subtract using a model.

   a) $\frac{1}{8} + \frac{1}{4}$ **b)** $\frac{1}{3} + \frac{1}{5}$ **c)** $\frac{5}{8} - \frac{1}{4}$

5. **a)** Find the equivalent fractions: $\frac{9}{10} = \frac{\blacksquare}{20}$ and $\frac{3}{4} = \frac{\blacksquare}{20}$

   b) Use the equivalent fractions to subtract $\frac{9}{10} - \frac{3}{4}$.

6. Solve using equivalent fractions.

   a) $\frac{1}{6} + \frac{1}{4}$ **b)** $\frac{3}{8} - \frac{1}{5}$ **c)** $\frac{5}{7} - \frac{1}{3}$

Adding and Subtracting Fractions Greater Than 1

▶ **GOAL: Solve problems by adding or subtracting mixed numbers and improper fractions.**

1. Model and solve.

   a) $3\frac{1}{5} + 2\frac{3}{5}$

   b) $1\frac{1}{2} + 3\frac{1}{4}$

   c) $3\frac{3}{4} - 1\frac{3}{8}$

   d) $9\frac{7}{10} - 4\frac{1}{5}$

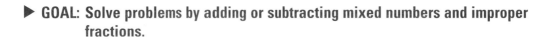

At-Home Help

These models can help you add and subtract fractions:

- number lines
- grids and counters
- fraction strips
- pattern blocks

2. Add.

   a) $1\frac{3}{4} + 2\frac{1}{4}$

   b) $3\frac{7}{10} + 1\frac{1}{10}$

   c) $2\frac{1}{8} + 3\frac{3}{8}$

   d) $5\frac{1}{2} + 3\frac{1}{4}$

   e) $\frac{5}{8} + 2\frac{1}{4}$

   f) $3\frac{3}{10} + 5\frac{2}{5}$

3. Subtract.

   a) $2\frac{7}{10} - 1\frac{3}{10}$

   b) $3\frac{5}{8} - 2\frac{3}{8}$

   c) $1\frac{5}{6} - \frac{1}{6}$

   d) $3\frac{7}{10} - 1\frac{1}{2}$

   e) $4\frac{3}{5} - 2$

   f) $1\frac{3}{8} - 1\frac{1}{8}$

4. Kayley used $1\frac{3}{4}$ cups of flour to make brownies. Hoshi used $2\frac{1}{8}$ cups of flour to make a cake. How much flour was used in total?

5. Reilly used $1\frac{7}{10}$ tubes of paint to paint a model. He used $2\frac{3}{8}$ tubes to finish an art project. How many tubes did he use in total?

6. On Saturday, it snowed for $4\frac{3}{4}$ h. On Sunday, it snowed for $1\frac{1}{2}$ h. How much longer did it snow on Saturday than on Sunday?

7. It took Rowyn $8\frac{1}{2}$ min to get up the ski slope and $1\frac{3}{4}$ min to get down. How much longer did it take Rowyn to go up?

8. Mei is planting tree seedlings. She started with $12\frac{1}{3}$ bags of seedlings, and then she planted $10\frac{3}{4}$ bags. How many bags does she have left to plant?

9. Calculate.

a) $1\frac{1}{4} + 4\frac{1}{3}$

d) $\frac{11}{4} + \frac{7}{6}$

g) $1\frac{2}{15} + \frac{4}{3}$

b) $2\frac{5}{8} - 2\frac{1}{2}$

e) $3\frac{1}{7} + 3\frac{1}{2}$

h) $8\frac{3}{4} - 6\frac{1}{9}$

c) $5\frac{8}{9} - 1$

f) $\frac{3}{2} - \frac{6}{5}$

i) $4\frac{7}{12} - 1\frac{1}{3}$

9.3 Exploring Fraction Patterns

▶ **GOAL: Analyze fraction patterns that involve addition and subtraction.**

1. Mei created the following fraction puzzle.

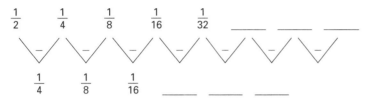

a) Fill in the missing fractions in Mei's puzzle.

b) Use words to describe the pattern in each row.

_____

_____

_____

2. Rowyn created the following fraction puzzle.

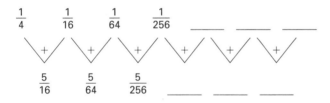

At-Home Help

When working with patterns, compare each term in the sequence with the term before. Ask yourself these questions to recognize the pattern:

• What fraction is added to or subtracted from each term to get the next term? How do these fractions relate to each other?

• Are any numbers in the sequence (such as the numerators of the terms) staying the same? Which ones?

• Are there any easily recognizable patterns (like 1, 2, 3, ... or 2, 4, 6, ...) in the numerators or denominators?

a) Fill in the missing fractions in Rowyn's puzzle.

b) Use words to describe the pattern in each row.

_____

_____

_____

c) Predict the 10th number in each row.

d) Write an algebraic expression to describe the *n*th term in each row.

9.4 Fractions of Fractions

▶ **GOAL: Represent one fraction as part of another fraction.**

1. Draw a model to show $\frac{1}{2}$ of $\frac{1}{2}$.

2. **a)** How does this picture show that $\frac{1}{4}$ of $\frac{1}{2}$ is $\frac{1}{8}$?

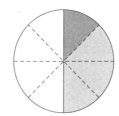

_____

_____

_____

b) How does this picture show that $\frac{1}{3}$ of $\frac{1}{4}$ is $\frac{1}{12}$?

_____

_____

_____

3. Draw a picture to show $\frac{2}{5}$ of $\frac{1}{3}$.

At-Home Help

To find a fraction of a fraction, start by drawing a model of the second fraction. For example, to find $\frac{1}{3}$ of $\frac{1}{2}$, start by drawing a model of $\frac{1}{2}$.

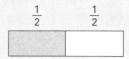

Next, divide each part of your model into further sections. Look at the first fraction to decide how many sections you will need. For example, divide each part of your model of $\frac{1}{2}$ into 3 to show thirds.

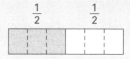

Now use a different colour to model the first fraction. For example, use a different colour to shade $\frac{1}{3}$ of $\frac{1}{2}$.

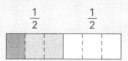

To find the answer, count how many sections of the whole are shaded with the new colour. In this example, one out of six sections is shaded, so $\frac{1}{3}$ of $\frac{1}{2}$ is $\frac{1}{6}$.

4. What are the missing fractions?

a) $\frac{1}{4}$ of $\frac{1}{3}$ is $\frac{\blacksquare}{12}$

b) $\frac{1}{4}$ of $\frac{2}{3}$ is $\frac{\blacksquare}{12}$, or $\frac{\blacksquare}{6}$

c) $\frac{3}{4}$ of $\frac{1}{6}$ is $\frac{3}{\blacksquare}$, or $\frac{1}{\blacksquare}$

9.5 Multiplying Fractions

▶ **GOAL: Multiply two fractions less than 1.**

1. Hoshi was asked to multiply $\frac{3}{4} \times \frac{2}{5}$. He solved the question in two ways: using a model, and by direct multiplication. However, the two answers he got did not match.

   Hoshi's Solution: "First, I used a model to solve the question. I drew a 4-by-5 grid. I shaded a rectangle that is $\frac{3}{4}$ of a unit wide and $\frac{2}{5}$ of a unit long."

"The shaded rectangle is made up of 6 small sections. There are 20 sections in total, so the answer is $\frac{6}{20}$, or $\frac{3}{10}$."

"Next, I solved the question by direct multiplication. I multiplied $\frac{2}{5}$ by 3 and by 4."

$$\frac{3}{4} \times \frac{2}{5} = \frac{3 \times 4 \times 2}{3 \times 4 \times 5}$$
$$= \frac{24}{60}$$
$$= \frac{6}{15}$$

a) What mistake did Hoshi make?

_____

_____

b) Which answer is correct? _____

2. What multiplication does each model represent?

   a)

   b)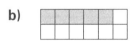

3. Draw a model for each multiplication and find each product.

a) $\frac{1}{4} \times \frac{4}{5}$

b) $\frac{1}{3} \times \frac{1}{3}$

c) $\frac{2}{3} \times \frac{4}{7}$

4. Calculate.

a) $\frac{2}{5} \times \frac{3}{5}$

d) $\frac{3}{4} \times \frac{5}{8}$

g) $\frac{3}{5} \times \frac{2}{7}$

b) $\frac{4}{7} \times \frac{3}{5}$

e) $\frac{1}{2} \times \frac{5}{8}$

h) $\frac{2}{5} \times \frac{3}{8}$

c) $\frac{3}{4} \times \frac{5}{7}$

f) $\frac{7}{8} \times \frac{3}{5}$

i) $\frac{3}{10} \times \frac{7}{8}$

5. The gas tank of a bus is $\frac{3}{4}$ full. A trip uses $\frac{1}{5}$ of the gas in the tank. What fraction of a tank is left after the trip?

6. Tinker is a fully grown cat. He eats $\frac{2}{3}$ of a can of cat food a day. How many cans of food does Tinker eat in a week?

7. Mei found $\frac{7}{8}$ of a package of crackers in the cupboard. She and her friends ate $\frac{3}{4}$ of the crackers. What fraction of the package did they eat?

Multiplying Fractions Greater Than 1

▶ **GOAL:** Multiply mixed numbers and improper fractions.

1. Estimate each product.

   a) $\frac{1}{3} \times 2\frac{1}{3}$

   c) $3\frac{5}{6} \times 3$

   b) $5\frac{1}{2} \times \frac{4}{5}$

   d) $2\frac{1}{8} \times 2\frac{1}{8}$

At–Home Help

One way of multiplying mixed numbers is to convert both numbers into improper fractions. For example:

$$2\frac{1}{3} \times 1\frac{3}{4} = \frac{7}{3} \times \frac{7}{4}$$

Next, multiply the two fractions.

$$\frac{7}{3} \times \frac{7}{4} = \frac{7 \times 7}{3 \times 4}$$
$$= \frac{49}{12}$$
$$= 4\frac{1}{12}$$

2. Use a model to find each product.

   a) $4\frac{1}{3} \times 1\frac{1}{5}$

   b) $3\frac{5}{6} \times 2\frac{1}{4}$

3. Calculate. Simplify your answer to lowest terms.

   a) $2\frac{1}{4} \times \frac{1}{2}$

   c) $3\frac{1}{3} \times 2\frac{1}{5}$

   e) $1\frac{3}{5} \times 6\frac{2}{3}$

   b) $1\frac{2}{5} \times 3\frac{1}{3}$

   d) $2\frac{1}{5} \times 4\frac{3}{8}$

   f) $60 \times 6\frac{1}{5}$

4. Teo takes $2\frac{1}{2}$ times as long to eat his lunch as Manuel. Manuel eats his lunch in 5 min. How long does Teo take?

9.7 Dividing Fractions I

▶ **GOAL:** Divide fractions using models and using equivalent fractions with a common denominator.

1. Calculate.

   a) $\frac{4}{5} \div \frac{2}{5}$

   c) $\frac{2}{3} \div \frac{1}{6}$

   e) $2 \div \frac{1}{3}$

   b) $\frac{18}{19} \div \frac{6}{19}$

   d) $\frac{1}{5} \div \frac{3}{10}$

   f) $\frac{9}{10} \div 3$

2. Draw a fraction strip model or a different picture to show the number of times $\frac{3}{5}$ fits into $\frac{7}{10}$.

At-Home Help

Try using common denominators when dividing fractions. For example:

$\frac{4}{5} \div \frac{1}{4}$

Change both fractions into equivalent fractions with a common denominator of 20.

$\frac{16}{20} \div \frac{5}{20}$

Divide the numerators to find out how many 5 twentieths fit into 16 twentieths.

$16 \div 5 = \frac{16}{5} = 3\frac{1}{5}$

The answer is a little more than 3.

3. Calculate.

   a) $\frac{9}{10} \div \frac{1}{5}$

   c) $\frac{7}{8} \div \frac{2}{3}$

   e) $\frac{2}{9} \div \frac{3}{5}$

   b) $\frac{1}{5} \div \frac{1}{2}$

   d) $\frac{1}{10} \div \frac{1}{6}$

   f) $\frac{6}{7} \div \frac{9}{10}$

4. Convert each mixed fraction into an improper fraction. Then calculate.

   a) $2\frac{1}{2} \div \frac{3}{4}$

   b) $1\frac{1}{2} \div 1\frac{2}{3}$

   c) $5\frac{2}{5} \div 2\frac{2}{3}$

5. Sheree knitted for $\frac{3}{4}$ h. If each row took her $\frac{1}{20}$ h, how many rows did she knit?

Dividing Fractions II

▶ **GOAL: Divide fractions using related multiplication.**

1. Write the reciprocal of each fraction.

a) $\frac{2}{5}$ d) $\frac{5}{6}$ g) $\frac{5}{8}$

b) $\frac{3}{4}$ e) $\frac{3}{10}$ h) $\frac{4}{5}$

c) $\frac{1}{2}$ f) $\frac{2}{3}$ i) $\frac{5}{1}$

2. Change each mixed number to an improper fraction. Then write the reciprocal of each fraction.

a) $1\frac{2}{3}$ d) $2\frac{3}{4}$ g) $2\frac{1}{3}$

b) $1\frac{3}{10}$ e) $3\frac{5}{6}$ h) $2\frac{5}{8}$

c) $2\frac{1}{4}$ f) $1\frac{9}{10}$ i) $4\frac{1}{6}$

3. Multiply each number by its reciprocal.

a) $\frac{3}{4}$ c) $\frac{1}{7}$

b) $\frac{8}{3}$ d) 3

> ### At–Home Help
>
> A **reciprocal** is the fraction that results from switching the numerator and denominator. For example, $\frac{4}{5}$ is the reciprocal of $\frac{5}{4}$.
>
> You can use reciprocals to divide fractions. For example:
>
> $$\frac{5}{6} \div \frac{2}{3}$$
>
> First, find the reciprocal of the second fraction (the divisor). The reciprocal of $\frac{2}{3}$ is $\frac{3}{2}$.
>
> Next, multiply the first fraction (the dividend) by the reciprocal.
>
> $$\frac{5}{6} \times \frac{3}{2} = \frac{5 \times 3}{6 \times 2}$$
> $$= \frac{15}{12}$$
> $$= \frac{5}{4}$$
> $$= 1\frac{1}{4}$$

4. Match each division with the corresponding multiplication, then find each answer.

a) $4 \div \dfrac{1}{2}$ b) $\dfrac{4}{5} \div 2$ c) $\dfrac{1}{2} \div \dfrac{3}{4}$ d) $\dfrac{5}{6} \div \dfrac{2}{3}$

A $\dfrac{1}{2} \times \dfrac{4}{3}$ B $\dfrac{5}{6} \times \dfrac{3}{2}$ C $\dfrac{4}{1} \times \dfrac{2}{1}$ D $\dfrac{4}{5} \times \dfrac{1}{2}$

5. Calculate.

a) $\dfrac{1}{5} \div \dfrac{2}{3}$ e) $\dfrac{4}{7} \div \dfrac{8}{21}$ i) $\dfrac{5}{6} \div \dfrac{2}{3}$

b) $\dfrac{3}{5} \div \dfrac{4}{7}$ f) $2 \div \dfrac{4}{5}$ j) $\dfrac{2}{7} \div \dfrac{1}{10}$

c) $\dfrac{5}{6} \div \dfrac{3}{5}$ g) $\dfrac{1}{2} \div 4$ k) $\dfrac{3}{8} \div 6$

d) $\dfrac{3}{10} \div \dfrac{4}{5}$ h) $\dfrac{1}{3} \div \dfrac{5}{3}$ l) $10 \div \dfrac{2}{5}$

6. Change any mixed numbers into improper fractions. Then calculate.

a) $1\dfrac{3}{4} \div \dfrac{2}{3}$ b) $4\dfrac{1}{3} \div \dfrac{1}{5}$ c) $3\dfrac{5}{6} \div 1\dfrac{1}{2}$

7. Teo has $4\dfrac{2}{3}$ pitchers of juice. One glass holds $\dfrac{1}{6}$ of a pitcher. How many glasses can Teo fill?

8. Manuel has $3\dfrac{1}{2}$ cans of paint. He needs $2\dfrac{1}{4}$ cans of paint to cover one wall. How many walls can he cover?

Communicating about Multiplication and Division

▶ **GOAL:** Describe the relationship between multiplying and dividing decimals and multiplying and dividing fractions.

1. Write the fraction equivalent for each decimal. If the fraction is not in lowest terms, simplify it.

   a) $0.75 =$ _____   **c)** $0.625 =$ _____

   b) $0.4 =$ _____   **d)** $0.50 =$ _____

2. Use the Communication Checklist to explain why $0.4 \div 0.2$ has the same answer as $4 \div 2$. (**Hint:** Convert the decimals into fractions with a denominator of 10.)

   _____

   _____

   _____

   _____

   _____

3. Draw a picture and write an explanation to show why $0.5 \times 2.6 = 1.3$.

   _____

   _____

   _____

   _____

   _____

4. Use the Communication Checklist to explain how to calculate $\frac{1}{4} \div \frac{1}{8}$ using reciprocal fractions.

   _____

   _____

   _____

   _____

9.10 Order of Operations

▶ **GOAL:** Understand the rules for order of operations, and apply them to fraction calculations.

1. Calculate.

a) $\dfrac{2}{3} + \dfrac{1}{4} - \dfrac{1}{6}$

d) $\dfrac{2}{3} \div \dfrac{4}{9} \times \dfrac{1}{2}$

b) $\dfrac{2}{3} - \dfrac{1}{2} + \dfrac{5}{6}$

e) $\dfrac{4}{5} + \dfrac{3}{10} \div \dfrac{3}{5}$

c) $\dfrac{3}{8} \times \dfrac{4}{5} \div \dfrac{9}{25}$

f) $\dfrac{1}{2} - \dfrac{3}{5} \times \dfrac{1}{6}$

At-Home Help

You can use the memory aid **BEDMAS** to remember the rules for order of operations.

Brackets

Exponents and square roots

Divide and **M**ultiply from left to right

Add and **S**ubtract from left to right

2. Fill in the blanks with >, <, or = to make each number sentence true.

a) $\dfrac{1}{2} - \left(\dfrac{1}{3} - \dfrac{1}{6}\right)$ _____ $\dfrac{3}{4} + \dfrac{2}{3} \div \dfrac{1}{4}$

c) $\left(\dfrac{5}{8} + \dfrac{1}{4}\right) \div \dfrac{1}{2}$ _____ $1\dfrac{1}{2} \div \dfrac{9}{10} - \dfrac{1}{3}$

b) $1\dfrac{3}{4} \times \dfrac{1}{4} + \dfrac{1}{2}$ _____ $\left(1\dfrac{1}{4} + \dfrac{1}{3}\right) - \dfrac{1}{3}$

d) $\left(\dfrac{1}{2} \div \dfrac{1}{3}\right) \div \dfrac{1}{4}$ _____ $1\dfrac{2}{5} \times \dfrac{3}{4} \div \dfrac{1}{2}$

3. Calculate.

a) $\left(\dfrac{1}{3} \div \dfrac{1}{4}\right) - \left(\dfrac{5}{2} \times \dfrac{1}{6}\right)$

c) $\left(\dfrac{1}{4} \times 4\right) \div \left(\dfrac{2}{3} + \dfrac{1}{4} \times \dfrac{1}{2}\right)$

b) $\left[\left(\dfrac{1}{2}\right)^2 + \dfrac{3}{4}\right] \div \dfrac{1}{3}$

d) $\left(\dfrac{3}{4} + \dfrac{2}{3} \div \dfrac{1}{4}\right) + \left(\dfrac{2}{3} \times \dfrac{3}{4} \div \dfrac{1}{2}\right)$

Test Yourself

1. Add or subtract using a model.

   a) $\dfrac{7}{8} - \dfrac{1}{8}$ c) $\dfrac{1}{5} - \dfrac{1}{10}$

   b) $\dfrac{3}{4} + \dfrac{3}{8}$ d) $\dfrac{1}{3} + \dfrac{5}{12}$

2. Use equivalent fractions to add or subtract.

   a) $\dfrac{1}{6} + \dfrac{1}{3}$ e) $\dfrac{6}{7} + \dfrac{1}{3}$

   b) $\dfrac{3}{4} - \dfrac{1}{8}$ f) $\dfrac{4}{5} - \dfrac{2}{3}$

   c) $\dfrac{5}{6} + \dfrac{1}{9}$ g) $\dfrac{1}{2} + \dfrac{5}{12}$

   d) $\dfrac{1}{10} - \dfrac{1}{20}$ h) $3 + \dfrac{1}{5}$

3. Jordan ate $\dfrac{1}{3}$ of the brownies, and Sheree ate $\dfrac{5}{8}$ of the brownies. Who ate the most brownies?

4. Model and solve.

   a) $3\dfrac{3}{4} - 2\dfrac{1}{8}$ b) $2\dfrac{1}{3} + 1\dfrac{1}{5}$

5. Calculate.

   a) $1\dfrac{1}{3} + 4\dfrac{2}{3}$ d) $4\dfrac{7}{8} - 3\dfrac{3}{4}$

   b) $5\dfrac{3}{8} - 2\dfrac{1}{8}$ e) $\dfrac{3}{5} + 3\dfrac{1}{6}$

   c) $2\dfrac{2}{3} + 1\dfrac{1}{6}$ f) $7\dfrac{4}{5} - 2\dfrac{1}{4}$

6. Teo found $2\dfrac{1}{5}$ packages of chocolate cookies and $3\dfrac{1}{2}$ packages of sugar cookies in the kitchen. How many packages of cookies did he find in total?

7. Draw a picture to show $\dfrac{1}{3}$ of $\dfrac{3}{4}$.

8. Draw a model for each multiplication and find the product.

   a) $\frac{1}{5} \times \frac{1}{2}$

   b) $\frac{5}{6} \times \frac{3}{4}$

9. Mei worked $\frac{3}{4}$ of last summer. She spent $\frac{1}{6}$ of that time babysitting, and $\frac{5}{6}$ of that time helping in her aunt's office.

   a) What fraction of the summer did Mei spend babysitting?

   b) What fraction of the summer did Mei spend helping in her aunt's office?

10. Calculate.

    a) $2\frac{1}{5} \times \frac{1}{6}$

    d) $4 \times 1\frac{2}{3}$

    b) $3\frac{3}{4} \times 1\frac{1}{7}$

    e) $\frac{5}{6} \times 10$

    c) $1\frac{7}{8} \times 2\frac{1}{6}$

    f) $\frac{3}{5} \times \frac{1}{10}$

11. Calculate.

    a) $\frac{5}{6} \div \frac{1}{6}$

    b) $\frac{1}{8} \div \frac{5}{8}$

12. Calculate.

    a) $6 \div \frac{1}{3}$

    d) $\frac{4}{5} \div 2$

    b) $2\frac{1}{3} \div \frac{1}{4}$

    e) $\frac{7}{8} \div \frac{2}{3}$

    c) $\frac{1}{8} \div \frac{1}{2}$

    f) $\frac{7}{10} \div \frac{4}{5}$

13. Manuel can read $4\frac{2}{3}$ pages in $2\frac{1}{2}$ min. How many pages can he read in 1 min?

14. Teo says that $\frac{8}{9} \div \frac{1}{3}$ is equal to one-third of $\frac{8}{9} \div \frac{1}{9}$. Do you agree? Explain why or why not.

    _____

    _____

    _____

    _____

15. Calculate.

    a) $\frac{5}{6} + \frac{1}{3} \times \frac{1}{2}$

    c) $\left(\frac{2}{3} + \frac{1}{4}\right)^2 \div 2$

    b) $\frac{9}{10} - \frac{1}{2} \div \frac{5}{7}$

    d) $\frac{6}{7} \div 5 + \frac{4}{5} \times 3$

10.1 Exploring Points on a Circle

▶ **GOAL: Locate the centre of a circle, given three points on the circle.**

1. List three pairs of lines in the diagram below that are perpendicular to each other.

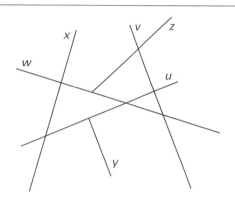

_____

2. **a)** In the diagram to the right, draw a line connecting points *A* and *B*. Draw a second line connecting points *B* and *C*.

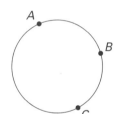

   b) Draw a perpendicular bisector of line *AB*.

   c) Draw a perpendicular bisector of line *BC*.

   d) Find the point where the two perpendicular bisectors meet. How do you know that this point is equidistant to points *A*, *B*, and *C*?

   _____

   _____

   _____

   _____

3. Use perpendicular bisectors to find the centre of the circle below.

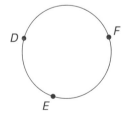

Intersecting Lines, Parallel Lines, and Transversals

▶ **GOAL:** Identify and apply the relationships between the measures of angles formed by intersecting lines.

1. What is the measure of each marked angle?

a)

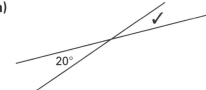

b)

c)

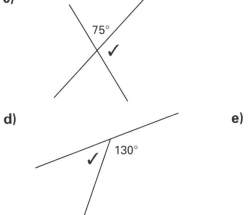

d) 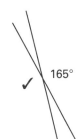   **e)**   **f)**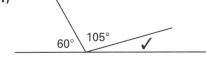

2. Fill in all the missing angles in the diagram.

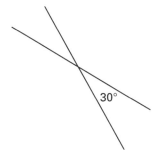

▶ **GOAL: Determine the sum of the angles in a triangle.**

1. Calculate the missing angle measures.

a)
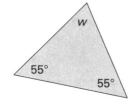

c)
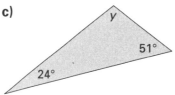

b)
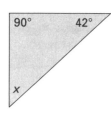

d)
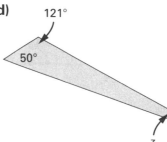

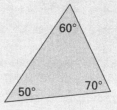
2. Calculate the missing angle measures.

a)
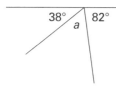

c)
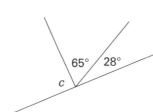

b)
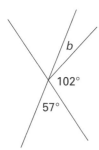

d)
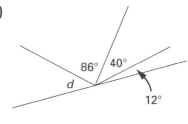

3. Two of the angles in a triangle measure 90° and 45°. What is the third angle?

_____

4. Two of the angles in a triangle add up to 80°. What is the third angle? _____

5. Nathan wants to draw a triangle with the angles 65°, 45°, and 75°. Is this possible? Explain why or why not.

_____

_____

10.4 Exploring Quadrilaterals

▶ **GOAL: Determine some angle properties of quadrilaterals.**

1. Determine the missing angles in each diagram.

a)

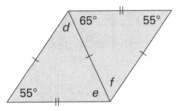

At-Home Help

Any quadrilateral can be divided into two triangles. You can use what you know about the angles of a triangle to calculate angles for quadrilaterals that are made from triangles. The angle sum in a quadrilateral is 360°.

b)

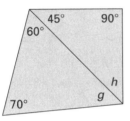

c)

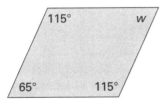

d)

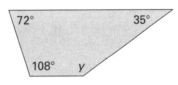

2. Determine the missing angles for each quadrilateral.

a)

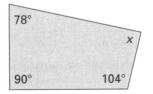

c)

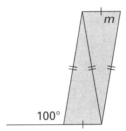

b)

d)

Exploring Right Triangles

▶ **GOAL: Relate the lengths of the sides of right triangles.**

1. A square has been constructed on each side of the right-angled triangles below. Calculate the area of each square. Then add the areas of the two smaller squares together.

a)

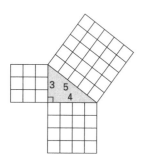

Area of largest square = _____

Area of smallest square + Area of next smallest square = _____

b)

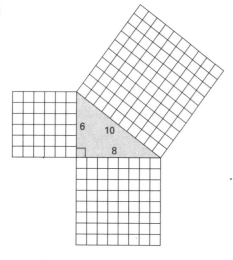

Area of largest square

= _____

Area of smallest square
+ Area of next smallest square

= _____

c)

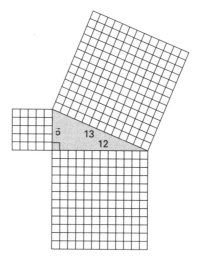

Area of largest square

= _____

Area of smallest square
+ Area of next smallest square

= _____

2. Write one or more sentences that describe the relationship between the areas of the squares drawn on the sides of the right-angled triangles.

_____

_____

10.6 Applying the Pythagorean Theorem

▶ **GOAL: Use the Pythagorean theorem to solve problems.**

1. Find the missing values. Use a calculator. Round your answers to one decimal place.

   a) $c^2 = 6^2 + 4^2$ $c =$ _____

   b) $12^2 = a^2 + 9^2$ $a =$ _____

   c) $4^2 + b^2 = 8^2$ $b =$ _____

   d) $a^2 + 5^2 = 9^2$ $a =$ _____

   e) $3^2 + 7^2 = c^2$ $c =$ _____

   f) $4^2 + b^2 = 9^2$ $b =$ _____

At-Home Help

A **hypotenuse** is the longest side of a right triangle, the side that is opposite the right angle.

The **Pythagorean theorem** states that the sum of the areas of the squares on the legs of a right triangle is equal to the area of the square on the hypotenuse.

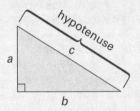

An equation for the Pythagorean theorem is $a^2 + b^2 = c^2$, where a and b are the lengths of the two smallest sides, and c is the length of the hypotenuse. You can use this equation to calculate the length of one side of a triangle, if you are given the other lengths.

2. For each diagram, calculate the area of the blank square.

   a)

   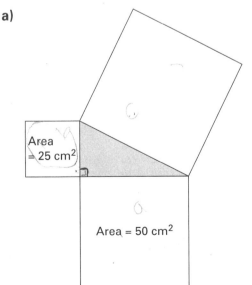

   Area = 25 cm²

   Area = 50 cm²

   b)

   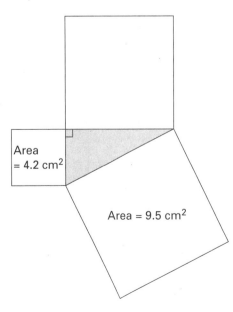

   Area = 4.2 cm²

   Area = 9.5 cm²

3. Calculate the length of the unknown side in each right triangle.

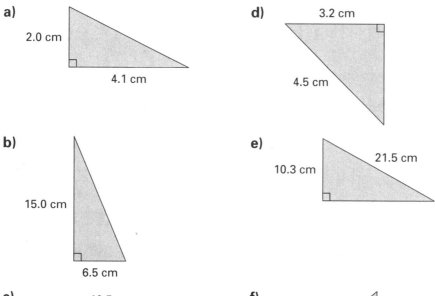

a)

2.0 cm

4.1 cm

d)

3.2 cm

4.5 cm

b)

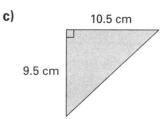

15.0 cm

6.5 cm

e)

10.3 cm

21.5 cm

c)

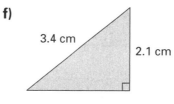

10.5 cm

9.5 cm

f)

3.4 cm

2.1 cm

4. Annika measured the sides of a right triangle to be 15 cm and 8 cm. Find the length of the hypotenuse.

5. Manuel and his brother sailed their boat from the marina 12 km north and 16 km east. How far are they from the marina?

6. A ladder is leaning against the side of a house. The ladder is 4.2 m long, and the base of the ladder is 1.3 m from the side of the house. How far up does the ladder reach? Draw a diagram, then solve the problem.

7. A rectangular swimming pool is 8.5 m long. The distance diagonally across the pool is 9.2 m. What is the area of the pool? Draw a diagram, then solve the problem.

10.7 Solve Problems Using Logical Reasoning

▶ **GOAL: Use logical reasoning to solve problems.**

1. The hypotenuse in a right triangle is 2.0 cm long. One leg of the triangle is 1.4 cm long. Is the triangle isosceles or scalene?

At–Home Help

Here are some tips that may help you solve logic problems.

- Ask yourself: What do I know? What do I need to find out?
- Rewrite the problem in your own words.
- Draw a diagram.
- Use a chart to organize the information.

2. Teo's house and Annika's house are both on Straight Street. Ken's house is on Park Street.

   - Park Street is perpendicular to Straight Street.
   - Park Street and Straight Street intersect exactly halfway between Teo's house and Annika's house.
   - Teo's house and Annika's house are 22.0 m apart.
   - Ken's house is 15.0 m away from the intersection of Park Street and Straight Street.

   What is the distance from Ken's house to Annika's house, travelling in a straight line?

3. Manuel, Rowyn, and Denis are playing Frisbee at the park. They left their jackets in a pile close by. Manuel is standing 5.3 m north of the pile of jackets. Rowyn is standing 2.5 m west of the jackets. Denis is standing 1.9 m east of the jackets.

   a) What is the distance between Manuel and Rowyn?

   b) What is the distance between Manuel and Denis?

Test Yourself

1. Look in the diagram below to find pairs of angles that match each description.

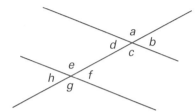

Adjacent angles: ____ and ____

Opposite angles: ____ and ____

Corresponding angles: ____ and ____

Supplementary angles: ____ and ____

2. Find the measure of each marked angle.

a)

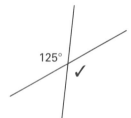

b)

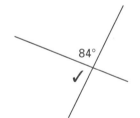

c)

d)

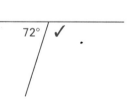

3. Find the measure of each marked angle.

a)

b)

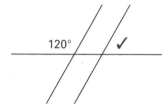

c)

d)

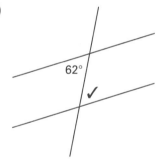

4. What are the measures of $\angle a$, $\angle b$, $\angle c$, and $\angle d$?

5. Calculate the missing angle measures in each triangle.

a)

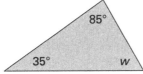

b)

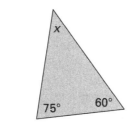

c)

d)

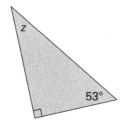

6. Calculate the missing angle measures in each quadrilateral.

a)

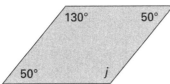

b)

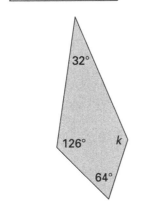

c)

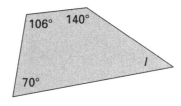

7. Calculate the length of the unknown side in each right triangle.

a)

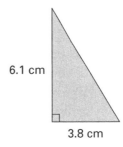

b)

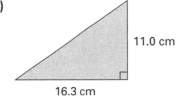

c)

d)

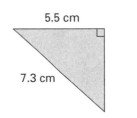

8. The angles in an isosceles triangles are 50° and 80°. What is the measure of the third angle?

9. A table is 4.1 m wide and 2.5 m long. What is the length of the diagonal across the table?

10. Denis is 9.2 m west of his house. The school is 23.0 m north of Denis' house. How far is Denis from the school, if he walks in a straight line?

▶ **GOAL: Explore the relationship between the dimensions of a cylinder and the dimensions of its net.**

1. Several nets of cylinders are shown below.

A. 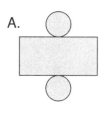 B. 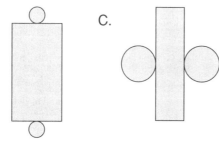 C.

D. 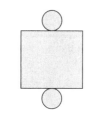 E.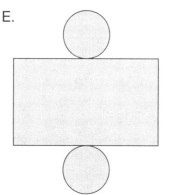

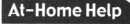
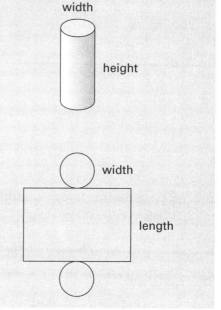
a) Put the cylinders in order from the tallest to the shortest.

_____

b) Put the cylinders in order from the widest to the narrowest.

_____

2. The base of a cylinder has a diameter of 10 cm and a circumference of 31.4 cm. The height of the cylinder is 22 cm. Use these dimensions to fill in the missing labels in the diagram.

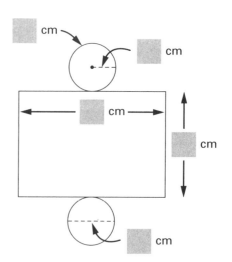

Surface Area of a Cylinder

▶ **GOAL: Develop and apply a formula for calculating the surface area of a cylinder.**

1. A cylinder is 12 cm tall and has a diameter of 3 cm. What is its surface area?

2. Use each net to estimate the surface area of the cylinder.

a)

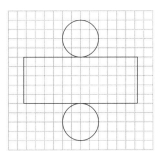

b)

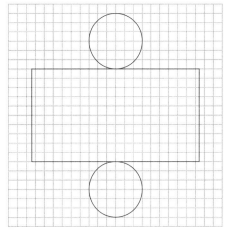

3. Calculate the surface area of each cylinder.

a)

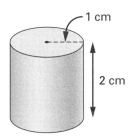

c)

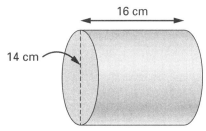

b)

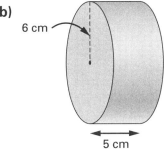

d)

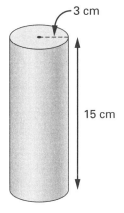

4. Use each net to determine the surface area of the cylinder.

a)

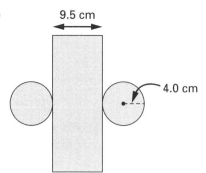

9.5 cm

4.0 cm

c)

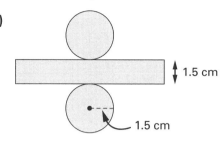

1.5 cm

1.5 cm

b)

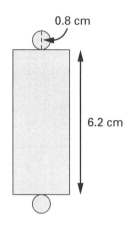

0.8 cm

6.2 cm

d)

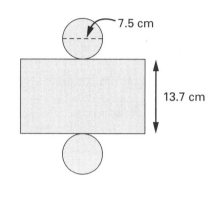

7.5 cm

13.7 cm

5. Calculate the surface area of each cylinder.

a)

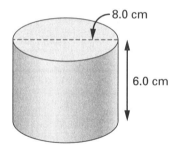

8.0 cm

6.0 cm

c)

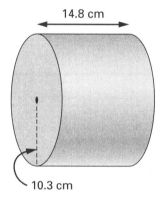

14.8 cm

10.3 cm

b)

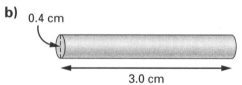

0.4 cm

3.0 cm

d)

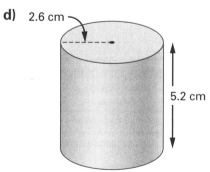

2.6 cm

5.2 cm

Volume of a Cylinder

▶ **GOAL: Develop and apply a formula for calculating the volume of a cylinder.**

1. Estimate the volume of each cylinder.

   a)

   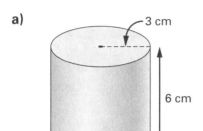

   b)

   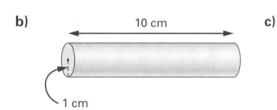

   c)

   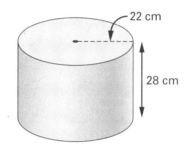

2. Calculate the volume of each cylinder.

   a)

   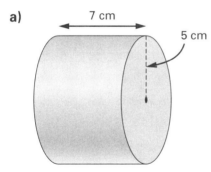

   c)

   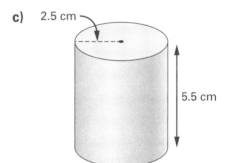

   b)

   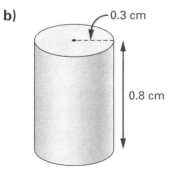

   d)

   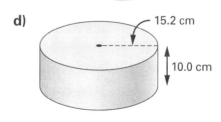

3. A cylinder has a radius of 5.0 cm and a volume of 1334.5 cm³. What is the height of the cylinder?

Solve Problems Using Diagrams

▶ **GOAL: Use diagrams to solve measurement problems.**

1. Find the volume of each figure.

a)

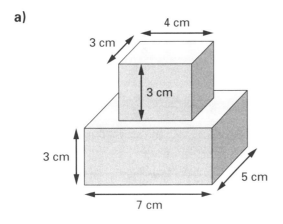

b)

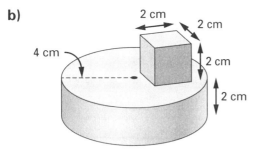

2. Calculate the surface area of the figure below.

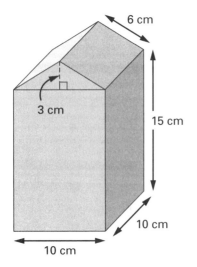

11.5 Exploring the Platonic Solids

▶ **GOAL: Investigate properties of the Platonic solids.**

1. The five Platonic solids are shown on this page, along with their nets. Fill out the table below to describe some of the properties of these solids. Some of the table has been filled in for you.

cube

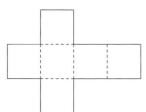

octahedron

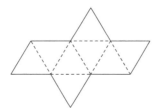

icosahedron

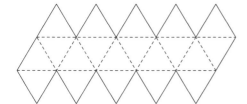

tetrahedron

dodecahedron

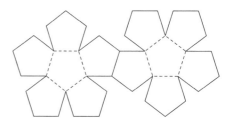

Polyhedron	Type of polygon	Number of faces (in total)	Number of vertices (in total)	Number of edges (in total)	Number of faces (at each vertex)
Tetrahedron	triangle				
Octahedron					4
Icosahedron		20		30	
Cube					
Dodecahedron			20	30	

11.6 Polyhedron Faces, Edges, and Vertices

▶ **GOAL:** Determine how the number of faces, edges, and vertices of a polyhedron are related.

1. A polyhedron has 6 faces and 4 vertices. Use Euler's formula to calculate the number of edges.

2. A polyhedron has 12 vertices and 22 edges. Use Euler's formula to calculate the number of faces.

3. Show that Euler's formula works for each polyhedron.

   a)

   c)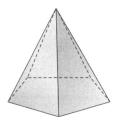

   b)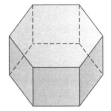

   d)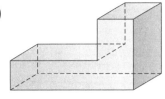

4. Tran says he is building a polyhedron with 5 vertices, 14 edges, and 11 faces. Benjamin says, "That's not possible." Who is correct? Why?

   _____

   _____

   _____

Test Yourself

1. Calculate the surface area of each cylinder.

   a)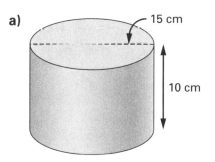
   15 cm
   10 cm

   b)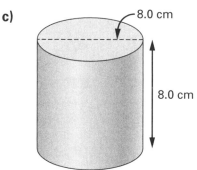
   1.5 cm
   2.8 cm

   c)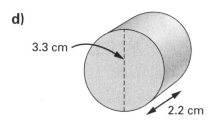
   8.0 cm
   8.0 cm

   d)
   3.3 cm
   2.2 cm

2. Use the net to find the surface area of the cylinder.

   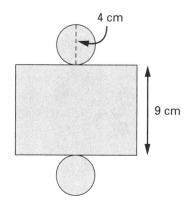
   4 cm
   9 cm

3. A cylinder has a radius of 15.5 cm and a height of 7.5 cm. Calculate the surface area.

4. Estimate which cylinder has the greatest volume.

   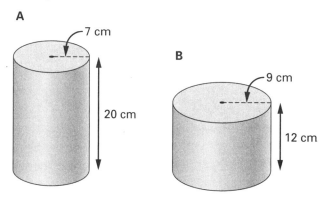
   A
   7 cm
   20 cm
   B
   9 cm
   12 cm

5. A circular swimming pool has a diameter of 7.4 m, and a height of 2.4 m. What is the volume of the pool?

6. Calculate the volume of each cylinder.

a)

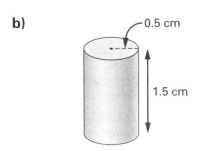

b)

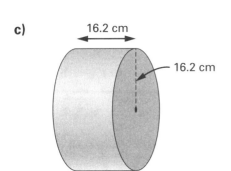

c)

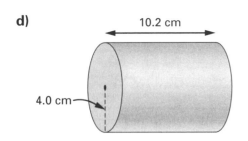

d)

7. Determine the volume of each object.

a)

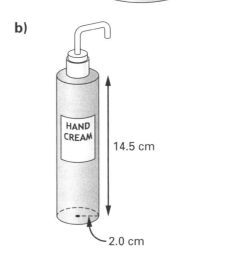

b)

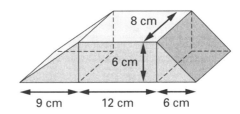

8. Calculate the volume of the figure below.

9. Show that Euler's formula works for the following figure.

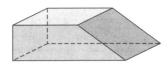

12.1 Exploring Theoretical and Experimental Probabilities

▶ **GOAL: Compare expected probability with the results of an experiment.**

1. What is the probability of each of the following events occurring?

   a) tossing a coin and getting heads _____

   b) a tree growing to be 6 km tall _____

   c) choosing one chocolate out of a box of four different chocolates without looking, and getting your favourite one _____

2. Jordan keeps eight different T-shirts in a drawer. If she reaches into the drawer without looking and pulls out a T-shirt, what is the probability that she will get the one she wants?

3. A weather station reports that there is a 40% chance of rain today. What is the probability that it will not rain today?

4. The faces on a number cube are numbered 1, 2, 3, 4, 5, and 6. The cube is rolled.

   a) What is the probability of rolling a 2? _____

   b) What is the probability of rolling an even number? _____

   c) What is the probability of rolling a prime number? _____

   d) What is the probability of rolling a 7? _____

5. A jar contains five blue marbles and four white marbles. If you reach in and take one marble without looking, what is the probability of the following?

   a) selecting a blue marble _____   **b)** selecting a white marble _____

6. Can the probability of an event ever be greater than 1? Explain your answer.

   _____

   _____

12.2 Theoretical and Experimental Probabilities

▶ **GOAL: Calculate and compare theoretical and experimental probabilities.**

1. Rishi has a paper bag with four green marbles, one red marble, and three white marbles. Calculate each theoretical probability if you reach in and take one marble.

   a) P(green) _____

   b) P(red) _____

   c) P(white) _____

2. Manuel reached into Rishi's bag and took out a marble. He recorded the colour, and then put it back. Manuel repeated this action eight times. His results are given in the table below.

	Green	Red	White
Try #1	✔		
Try #2		✔	
Try #3	✔		
Try #4	✔		
Try #5			✔
Try #6		✔	
Try #7	✔		
Try #8			✔
Total	4	2	2

Use the data in Manuel's table to calculate each experimental probability.

   a) P(green) _____

   b) P(red) _____

   c) P(white) _____

3. Was Manuel's experimental probability close to the theoretical probability you calculated in question 1? Explain your answer.

   _____

   _____

   _____

12.3 Calculating Probabilities

▶ **GOAL: Use tree diagrams and organized lists to calculate probabilities.**

1. a) Complete the tree diagram to show the possible outcomes for tossing two coins.

First coin	Second coin	Outcome
heads	heads ──▶	H–H
	▢ ──▶	▢
tails	▢ ──▶	▢
	tails ──▶	▢

b) How many possible outcomes are there? _____

c) What is *P*(two heads)? _____

d) What is *P*(one heads and one tails)? _____

2. You have two spinners as shown below.

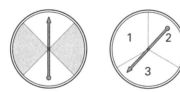

a) Both spinners are spun. Use a tree diagram to list all the possible outcomes.

> ### At-Home Help
>
> A **favourable outcome** is a desired result when calculating probability. To find the probability of an event, compare the number of favourable outcomes to the total number of possible outcomes.
>
> | 1st child | 2nd child | Outcome |
> |---|---|---|
> | boy | boy | B–B |
> | | girl | B–G |
> | girl | boy | G–B |
> | | girl | G–G |
>
> You can use a tree diagram to determine possible outcomes. For example, suppose you want to know the probability of a family having two children, and both being girls. The tree diagram below shows the possible outcomes.
>
> The favourable outcome is G-G, or two girls. Comparing the number of favourable outcomes (1) to the number of possible outcomes (4) gives the following probability: 1 out of 4, or $\frac{1}{4}$.

b) How many possible outcomes are there? _____

c) What is *P*(grey and number 2)? _____

Copyright © 2006 by Nelson Education Ltd.

Chapter 12: Probability **123**

3. Kito is given a white die and a red die. He will roll both dice, and then count the number of dots on the upper face of each die.

   a) Complete Kito's chart of possible outcomes. **W** means the number of dots on the white die, and **R** means the number of dots on the red die.

(W,R)	(W,R)	(W,R)	(W,R)	(W,R)	(W,R)
(1, 1)	(2, 1)	(3, 1)			
(1, 2)	(2, 2)				
(1, 3)					

   b) How many possible outcomes are there? _____

   c) What is *P*(6, 6)? _____

   d) What is *P*(both numbers 3 or greater)? _____

   e) What is *P*(one 2 and one 4, in any order)? _____

4. On her vacation, Carina brought three shirts (blue, white, and pink) and two pairs of shorts (denim and khaki).

   a) Draw a tree diagram to show the different possible outfits Carina could wear.

   b) If Carina chooses an outfit randomly, what is *P*(white shirt, khaki shorts)? _____

5. Kayley's family has two boys and one girl. What is the probability of this happening? Use a tree diagram to solve the problem.

Solve Problems Using Organized Lists

▶ **GOAL: Use an organized list to solve a problem.**

1. Kito has four coins in his pocket. He says they are a combination of quarters, dimes, and nickels.

   At-Home Help

   When using an organized list, look for patterns in your chart or table. This will help you to be sure that you did not miss or repeat any combinations.

   a) Complete the table below to find all the possible combinations of coins.

Quarters	Dimes	Nickel	Total
4	0	0	$1.00
3	1	0	
3	0	1	
2			
2			
2			
1			
1			
1			
1			
0			
0			
0			
0			
0			

   b) What pattern do you see in the organized list? _____

   _____

   c) Kito says the coins add up to $0.40. If you are given only one guess, what is the probability that you will guess the correct combination of coins?

2. Carina has three marbles in a bag: a white one, a red one, and a green one. She takes the marbles out one at a time and records the order of the colours. What is the probability that Carina will take the marbles out in this order: red, green, white?

Using Simulations to Determine Probability

▶ **GOAL: Choose a model to determine the probability of a real-life event.**

1. When a coin is tossed, the theoretical probability of getting heads is $\frac{1}{2}$, or 0.5. Rowyn wanted to find out if the experimental probability was the same as the theoretical probability. She tossed a coin 50 times and recorded her results: 23 heads and 27 tails.

   a) What is the experimental probability of tossing heads?

   b) What is the experimental probability of tossing tails?

2. **a)** Jordan's parents are planning to have two more children. What is the theoretical probability that both children will be girls?

   b) Which model would you choose to calculate the experimental probability that both children will be girls? Explain your answer.
   - rolling a die
   - tossing a coin
   - spinning a spinner divided into four parts

   _____

   _____

   c) Use your model to carry out a simulation. Then calculate the experimental probability.

   d) How does your experimental probability compare to the theoretical probability you calculated in part (a)?

   _____

12.6 Designing a Probability Model

▶ **GOAL: Design a probability model to simulate a real-life event.**

1. Annika usually gets four out of five serves over the net in volleyball. She knows she will have six chances during gym class to serve the ball, and she wants to know the probability that she will get all six serves over the net.

a) Describe a model you could use to find the experimental probability that Annika will get all six serves over the net.

_____

_____

b) Write out the steps to explain how to use this model to find the experimental probability.

_____

_____

_____

_____

_____

_____

c) Perform your simulation and record your results.

d) Use your results to calculate the experimental probability of Annika getting all six serves over the net.

Test Yourself

1. Calculate the theoretical probability for each situation.

   a) tossing a coin and getting heads

   b) rolling a die and getting a 2

   c) choosing 1 card out of a deck of 52 and getting a diamond.

2. A bag holds six marbles: one red, two blue, and three black. Calculate each probability if you reach into the bag without looking and take out one marble.

   a) P(red)

   b) P(blue)

   c) P(white)

3. There are 5 quarters, 7 dimes, and 12 nickels in a piggy bank. You take one coin without looking. Calculate each probability.

   a) P(quarter)

   b) P(dime)

   c) P(nickel)

4. The letters in the word "garden" are printed on six cards. The cards are shuffled and turned down.

   a) If you pick one card, what are the possible outcomes?

   _____

   _____

   b) What is the probability of picking each outcome?

   c) What is the probability of picking a consonant?

   d) What is the probability of picking a vowel?

5. Carina rolled an eight-sided die (with numbers 1 to 8) 32 times. She used her results to calculate the following experimental probabilities:

   $P(5) = \dfrac{5}{32}$

   $P(\text{even number}) = \dfrac{16}{32}$

   $P(\text{less than 3}) = \dfrac{7}{32}$

   Which experimental probability matches the theoretical probability exactly?

6. Kito has three pairs of shoes (brown, black, and red) and six pairs of socks (white, black, blue, brown, beige, green).

a) Draw a tree diagram to show all the different combinations of shoes and socks Kito can wear.

b) If he chooses his shoes and socks randomly, what is the probability that Kito will wear green socks with red shoes?

c) What is the probability that Kito will wear shoes and socks that are the same colour?

7. Jordan has three bills in her wallet. They might be any combination of $5, $10, and/or $20 bills.

a) Fill in the organized list to show all the possible combinations of bills.

$5	$10	$20	Total

b) Jordan says the bills add up to $30. If you take one guess, what is the probability that you can guess what the bills are?

8. The weather report says there is a 33% chance of rain every day this week. Rowyn wants to find the experimental probability that it will rain every day for the next three days. She sets up an experiment using this spinner.

a) Describe how Rowyn can use the spinner to find the experimental probability that it will rain every day for the next three days.

_____

_____

_____

_____

_____

b) Rowyn recorded her results in the following table. Use her results to calculate the experimental probability that it will rain every day for the next three days.

Rain on all three days	Rain on two days or less
III	HH HH HH HH HH HH HH HH HH HH HH HH HH HH HH HH HH HH I

Answers

Chapter 1

1.1 Identifying Prime and Composite Numbers

1. 2, 3, 5, 7, 11, 13, 17, 19
2. The number ends in 0, so it is divisible by 5 and by 10.
3. a) composite: 1, 3, 7, 21
   b) prime
   c) composite: 1, 3, 11, 33
   d) composite: 1, 3, 13, 39
   e) composite: 1, 3, 17, 51
   f) prime
4. a) No, it is composite.
   b) The area of the park can be divided by itself, 1, 17, and 11.

1.2 Prime Factorization

1. a) The missing factor is 3; $18 = 2 \times 3 \times 3$
   b) The missing factors are 45 and 5; $225 = 3 \times 3 \times 5 \times 5$
2. a) 5×19
   b) $2 \times 2 \times 2 \times 2 \times 7$
   c) $2 \times 2 \times 41$
   d) $2 \times 3 \times 5 \times 5$
3. a) 2 b) 3 c) 7 d) 5 e) 23 f) 3 g) 13 h) 3
4.
```
        119
       /   \
      7     17
```
5.
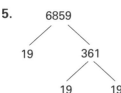
```
      6859
     /    \
    19     361
          /   \
         19    19
```

1.3 Common Factors and Common Multiples

1. b) 25 and 750 c) 40 and 240 d) 10 and 2100
   e) 50 and 150
2. Possible answers include the following:
   a) 2, 7, 14 and 84, 168, and 252
   b) 5, 10, 25 and 350, 700, and 1050
   c) 8, 12, 24 and 144, 288, and 432
   d) 4, 6, 12 and 264, 528, and 792
3. a) 15 and 90 b) 5 and 350 c) 18 and 252
   d) 21 and 252

4. 111 m
5. a) $0.75
   b) Tamara bought four, Teo bought five.
6. four tennis balls
7. In 30 days

1.4 Calculating Powers

1. a) base: 3, exponent: 7 b) base: 10, exponent: 8 c) base: 1, exponent: 3
2. a) $7 \times 7 \times 7$
   b) $12 \times 12 \times 12 \times 12 \times 12$
   c) $4 \times 4 \times 4 \times 4 \times 4 \times 4$
   d) $25 \times 25 \times 25 \times 25$
3. a) 2^9 b) 9^4 c) 21^5 d) 103^6
4. a) $3^2 = 9$ b) $2^3 = 8$ c) $5^2 = 25$ d) $4^3 = 64$
   e) $3^4 = 81$ f) $2^5 = 32$
5. a) 2187 b) 6561 c) 20 736 d) 390 625
   e) 0.031 25 f) 0.456 533 g) 39.69 h) 8615.125
6. a) $0.7 \times 0.7 \times 0.7 \times 0.7 = 0.2401$
   b) $11 \times 11 \times 11 = 1331$
   c) $1.3 \times 1.3 = 1.69$
   d) $99 \times 99 \times 99 \times 99 = 96\ 059\ 601$
7. a) $4^4 = 256$ b) $6^6 = 46\ 656$ c) $13^3 = 2197$
   d) $3^7 = 2187$
8. a) < b) < c) < d) > e) > f) > g) < h) > i) <
9. 531 441 pieces of paper
10. 6561 elastic bands
11. seven times

1.5 Expanded Form and Scientific Notation

1. a) 2 b) 3 c) 2 d) 6
2. a) 10^2, 10, 1 b) 10^3, 10^2, 10, 1 c) 2, 0, 8 d) 430
3. b) 3481, 3.481×10^3
   c) 7110, $7 \times 10^3 + 1 \times 10^2 + 1 \times 10$
   d) $9 \times 10^3 + 8 \times 10^2 + 5 \times 10 + 4 \times 1$, 9.854×10^3
   e) 88 030, $8 \times 10^4 + 8 \times 10^3 + 3 \times 10$
   f) $1 \times 10^4 + 7 \times 10^2 + 7 \times 10 + 2 \times 1$, 1.0772×10^4
   g) 109 005, $1.090\ 05 \times 10^5$
   h) 60 300, $6 \times 10^4 + 3 \times 10^2$
4. a) < b) > c) >

1.6 Square Roots

1. a) 3 b) 5 c) 7 d) 8 e) 9 f) 11 g) 20 h) 60

2. **b)** 8.1 **c)** 4.9 **d)** 10.1 **e)** 3.2 **f)** 5.9
3. **a)** 4.359 **b)** 5.745 **c)** 9.220 **d)** 11.747 **e)** 27.148
   f) 22.091
4. 25 m $\times$ 25 m

1.7 Exploring Square Roots and Squares

1. **a)** 3 cm **b)** 9 cm^2 **c)** 4.243 cm
2. **a)** 36 cm^2 **b)** 64 m^2 **c)** 121 cm^2
3. **a)** 8.485 cm **b)** 11.314 m **c)** 15.556 cm
4. **a)** 7 cm **b)** 12 cm **c)** 15 m
5. **a)** 9.899 cm **b)** 16.971 cm **c)** 21.213 m

1.8 Order of Operations

1. **a)** Selena did not do all the multiplication
      first before starting to add.
   b) Nathan started by adding.
   c) 9
2. **a)** $(5 - 1) \times 6 = 24$
   b) $12 \div (4 - 1) = 4$
   c) $(3 + 4) \times (6 - 5) = 7$
   d) $(6 + 8) \div 2 = 7$
   e) $(1 + 2)^2 = 9$
   f) $20 - (3 \times 2 + 5) = 9$
3. **a)** 44 **b)** 17 **c)** 80 **d)** 270 **e)** 100 **f)** 3
4. **a)** 20 **b)** 23 **c)** 75 **d)** 5 **e)** 12.5 **f)** 81 **g)** 2 **h)** 3
5. $(15 + 22 + 53) \div (12 + 18) = 3$
6. $4 \times 12 + 6 \times 8 = 96$

1.9 Communicating about Number Problems

1. **a)** 5.91×10^9 km **b)** 4.1685×10^3 min
2. **a)** 5.9737×10^{24} kg **b)** 7.3749×10^{22} kg

Test Yourself

1. **a)** neither
   b) prime
   c) composite: 1, 3, 7, 21
   d) composite: 1, 5, 17, 85
   e) prime
   f) composite: 1, 2, 19, 38
2. **a)** $78 = 2 \times 3 \times 13$
   b) $675 = 3 \times 3 \times 3 \times 5 \times 5$
   c) $1092 = 2 \times 2 \times 3 \times 7 \times 13$
   d) $660 = 2 \times 2 \times 3 \times 5 \times 11$
   e) $567 = 3 \times 3 \times 3 \times 3 \times 7$
   f) $1372 = 2 \times 2 \times 7 \times 7 \times 7$
3. **a)** 3 and 132 **b)** 6 and 126 **c)** 20 and 880
   d) 1 and 285
4. **a)** $9^3 = 729$ **b)** $3^7 = 2187$ **c)** $0.5^4 = 0.063$
   d) $5.3^6 = 22\ 164.361$
5. **a)** $2 \times 2 \times 2 \times 2 \times 2 \times 2 \times 2 \times 2 = 256$
   b) $4 \times 4 \times 4 \times 4 = 256$
   c) $8.1 \times 8.1 \times 8.1 \times 8.1 \times 8.1 = 34\ 867.844$
   d) $7 \times 7 \times 7 \times 7 \times 7 \times 7 \times 7 \times 7 \times 7 =$
      40 353 607

6. **a)** $8 \times 10^3 + 8 \times 10^2 + 8 \times 10 + 4 \times 1$
   b) $1 \times 10^4 + 9 \times 10^3 + 2 \times 10^2 + 3 \times 1$
   c) $2 \times 10^4 + 2 \times 10^3$
7. **a)** 7.32×10^2 **b)** 9.404×10^3 **c)** 8.4914×10^4
   d) 1.73002×10^6
8. **a)** > **b)** > **c)** > **d)** >
9. **a)** 5.9 **b)** 5.1 **c)** 2.1 **d)** 3.2
10. **a)** 3.9 **b)** 6.6 **c)** 22.4 **d)** 47.7
11. 6159 km
12 **a)** 15 **b)** 8 **c)** 108 **d)** 3375 **e)** 35 **f)** 4 **g)** 3 **h)** 10

Chapter 2

2.1 Expressing Fractions as Decimals

1. **a)** $0.\overline{6}$ **b)** $0.\overline{09}$ **c)** $0.\overline{142\ 853\ 7}$
2. (a), (c), and (d) repeat: **a)** 0.1666... **b)** 0.3
   c) 0.285 714 285 714... **d)** 0.7272...
3. **a)** < **b)** < **c)** < **d)** > **e)** < **f)** >
4. **a)** terminating **b)** repeating **c)** repeating
   d) terminating **e)** repeating **f)** terminating
   g) repeating **h)** terminating **i)** repeating

2.2 Multiplying and Dividing Decimals

1. **a)** 14.4 **b)** 9.24 **c)** 38.85 **d)** 175.75 **e)** 430
   f) 2.609 523 81
2. **a)** 0.35 **b)** 33.18 **c)** 2.1 **d)** 0.0861 **e)** 0.322 **f)** 48
   g) 5.491 **h)** 183.372
3. **a)** 0.9 **b)** 0.4 **c)** 0.7 **d)** 0.08 **e)** 3.9 **f)** 1.6 **g)** 5.5
   h) 12.4
4. $131.63
5. 3.04 kg
6. 28 figurines
7. **a)** 100 lake trout
   b) 2714.4 kg for 4 tuna, or 2950 kg for 100
      lake trout
8. **a)** $3.12 **b)** $0.61
9. $2.80
10. 18.6 km/h

2.3 Exploring Ratios

1. **a)** 3:3 **b)** 8:1 **c)** 1:8 **d)** 7:8 **e)** 24:40
2. **a)** 4:3 **b)** 1:3 **c)** 2:4 **d)** 3:2:1
3. Your pattern should have 12 squares in one
   colour, and 4 squares in a different colour.

2.4 Ratios

1. **a)** 2 **b)** 2 **c)** 6 **d)** 15 **e)** 2 **f)** 3
2. **a)** 5 **b)** 2 **c)** 6 **d)** 10
3. **a)** 10, scale factor: 2
   b) 15, scale factor: 5
   c) 1.5, scale factor: 0.5
   d) 6.3, scale factor: 3

e) 24, scale factor: 0.125

f) 4.6, 9, scale factor: 3.2

4. 3 : 0.75, or 180 : 45
5. 40 homes
6. 28 times

2.5 Rates

1. a) $12.21/h b) $12.67/CD c) 12 km/h d) 60 m/s
   e) $0.40/bottle f) $133/week g) $0.75/can
   h) 80 km/h i) $7.78/kg
2. a) $11.25/h b) $450.00
3. a little over 14 bicycles
4. 240 words
5. $81.00
6. 2250 mm, or 2.25 m

2.6 Representing Percent

1. a) 25% b) 75% c) 40% d) 110% e) 80%
2. a) 75% b) 25% c) 60% d) 90% e) 20%
3. a) 272 pupils b) 68 pupils
4. a) $15 b) $32 c) $110.50 d) $340
5. six items of clothing
6. a) 4 pizzas
   b) 1 tub of ice cream
   c) 27 cupcakes
   d) 6 bags of chips

2.7 Solving Percent Problems

1. a) 25 b) 75 c) 1 d) 42 e) 25 f) 12
2. 65%
3. 60%
4. 84 CDs
5. 18 times
6. 87.5%
7. about 15%
8. 10.8 h
9. 472.2 km
10. 6200 bolts
11. 50 cards
12. 40 pitches
13. $600
14. $90

2.8 Solving Percent Problems Using Decimals

1. $184.54
2. a) $4.50 b) $20.00 c) $24.38 d) $27.46
3. $14.77
4. a) $40.46 b) $11.24
5. $241.49

2.9 Solve Problems by Changing Your Point of View

1. a) Nathan reasons that the sale price is equal to the regular price minus the discount, or 100% of the price minus 20% of the price. Instead of finding the discount and subtracting it, he finds 80% of the price. To do this, he multiplies the price by 0.80.
   b) Jordan reasons that the sale price is equal to 90% of the regular price. [See the reasoning in part (a).] So the sale price equals $95 × 0.90. She also reasons that the final purchase price is equal to 100% of the sale price plus 15% of the sale price, or 115% of the sale price. So the final purchase price is equal to (sale price) × 1.15, or ($95 × 0.90) × 1.15.
2. a) $130.30 b) $66.15

Test Yourself

1. a) 0.25 b) 0.7 c) 0.375 d) 0.34 e) 0.5625
   f) 0.828 125
2. a) $0.\overline{6}$ b) $0.\overline{857\ 142}$ c) $0.08\overline{3}$ d) $0.\overline{5}$ e) $0.\overline{904\ 761}$
   f) $0.\overline{36}$
3. a) terminates b) repeats c) repeats
   d) terminates e) terminates f) repeats
4. a) 8.8 b) 32.13 c) 3.81 d) 1.375 e) 57.8125
   f) 0.04375
5. $329.38
6. a) 4 b) 30 c) 9 d) 2, 4 e) 3, 15 f) 20, 7
7. 17.28 km
8. a) $2.80 b) $1.95 c) $17.13 d) $25.97 e) $3.49
   f) $5936.26
9. 6 c flour, $1\frac{1}{2}$ c butter (or 1.5 c butter), and 3 c sugar
10. a) 412 b) 242 c) 340
11. a) 15 b) 93.75% c) 275 d) 34.2 e) 86% f) 625
12. seven classmates
13. 42.5%
14. a) $44.52 b) $133.56
15. $53.06
16. a) $151.69 b) $32.81

Chapter 3

3.1 Organizing and Presenting Data

1. a) a bar graph or a stem-and-leaf plot are appropriate
   b) 58%
   c) 42%
   d) A playing field makes most sense, since more students will use it.

3.2 Exploring Sample Size

1. **a)** Once tested, popcorn cannot be sold.
   b) Taking a sample is much easier and less time-consuming than compiling data from every family in the country.
   c) Once tested, light bulbs cannot be sold.
2. **a)** census **b)** sample **c)** census **d)** sample
   e) sample
3. **a)** census; you can ask every student in the class
   b) sample; once tested, a battery cannot be sold

3.3 Using Electronic Databases

1.

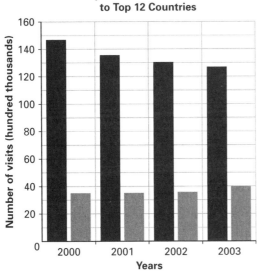

Comparison of Canadian Visits to Top 12 Countries

2. decreasing
3. increasing
4. U.S.A., Mexico, U.K., France, Cuba
5. 76.2%
6. 0.7%

3.4 Histograms

1. **a)** bar graph **b)** histogram **c)** histogram
   d) bar graph **e)** bar graph
2. **a)**

Age	10–20	20–30	30–40	40–50	50–60	60–70
Frequency	4	7	9	12	3	1

b)

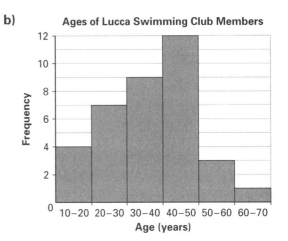

Ages of Lucca Swimming Club Members

3. **a)**

Time (min)	6.5–7.0	7.0–7.5	7.5–8.0	8.0–8.5	8.5–9.0	9.0–9.5	9.5+
Frequency	2	4	8	5	2	2	1

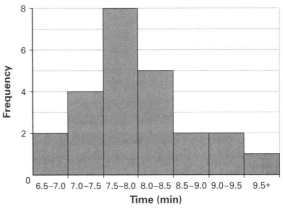

Biking Times Over a 2 km Distance

4. **a)** 20 plants
   b) No, you can't use the histogram to find any specific heights. Because the data is organized in intervals, you can only find the approximate height of any plant.
   c) Based on Benjamin's data, they would be most likely to grow to 12−14 cm.

3.5 Mean, Median, and Mode

1. **a)** 8.3, 8, and none **b)** 7.5, 5.5, and 5 **c)** 4.3, 3, and 3 **d)** 15.3, 15, and both 14 and 15
   e) 35, 35.5, and none **f)** 107.5, 107, and none
2. **a)** 4.3, 3.4
   b) 4,1, 3.4; the mean changed the most

3. a)

Stem	Leaf
0	1 2 4 5 7 8 9
1	2 3 5 8
2	3 6 7
3	1 4 8
4	1 3 6
5	
6	4 5
7	4
8	3

   b) 28.7 and 24.5

   c) 26.3 and 23

   d) the mean changed the most

4. 18.7, 19, and 20

5. a) No, 23 does not have to be one of the data values. For example, the set of data 21, 22, 24, 25 has the mean 23 but 23 is not one of the values.

   b) For example, 21, 22, 23, 24, 25

   c) For example, 21, 22, 24, 25

6. a) No, 23 does not have to be one of the data values. For example, the set of data 15, 20, 26, 28 has a median that is 20 + 26 ÷ 2, or 23.

   b) For example, 14, 18, 23, 28, 42

   c) For example, 15, 20, 26, 28

3.6 Communicating about Graphs

1. a)

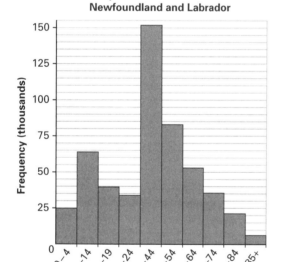

b) The data is organized to be most useful for a researcher. For example, preschool children (0–5), high school students (15–19), and college or university

students (20–24) each have their own categories. Adults in the middle of their careers (25–44) also have their own category.

c) Your answer might be something like this: "I chose to display the data using a histogram, because the data is organized into intervals. According to the data and my graph, 63.9 thousand out of 512.8 thousand people in Newfoundland and Labrador are between the ages of 5–14. This is equal to 12.5%. I can assume that the population of Stefan's new town follows the same pattern. Therefore, 12.5% of the population of the town will go to the junior middle school. 12.5% of 1720 is equal to 215. There will be 215 students at the school."

Test Yourself

1. a) 120 students

   b) 25%

   c)

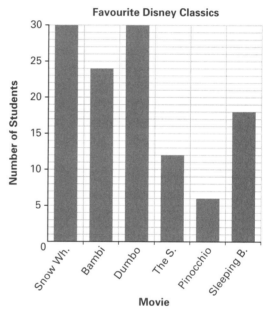

d) The graph clearly shows that *Snow White, Bambi,* and *Dumbo* are the top favourites.

2. a) The survey was a census since it included every student in the school.

   b) 53% and 10%

   c) The percent in Rishi's class are reasonably close to the school percent, but they are not the same. Each class will have a slightly different distribution of hair colour.

3.

Average Heights of Plants Grown in Two Types of Light

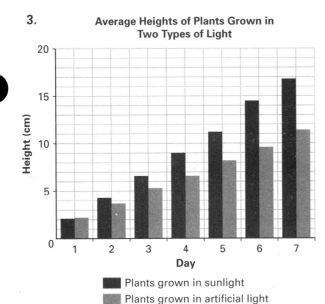

Plants grown in sunlight
Plants grown in artificial light

4. a)

Interval (s)	Frequency
6.0–6.9	6
7.0–7.9	11
8.0–8.9	6
9.0–9.9	4
10.0–10.9	3

b)

Running Times for 50 m Race

c) 7.4 s and 7.5 s

d) This histogram shows that more than half of the students have a time of 7.9 s or less.

Chapter 4

4.1 Exploring Relationships in the Fibonacci Sequence

1. 55, 89, 144, 233, 377, 610

2. a) 105 **b)** 104 **c)** 1

3. For four consecutive Fibonacci numbers, the difference between (greatest number × least number) and (first middle number × second middle number) is always 1.

4. a) For example, 5, 8, 13, and 21
b) 4.2
c) 4.2, 4.2, 4.2; The number is always 4.2.

5. Other patterns include: (1) for three consecutive numbers, the difference between (greatest number × least number) and (middle number)^2 is always 1; and (2) for six consecutive numbers, the difference between (two greatest numbers × two least numbers) and (first middle number × second middle number)^2 is always less than 1.

4.2 Creating Pattern Rules from Models

1. a) shade the top square in each figure
b) shade the square on the right in each figure
c) shade the two triangles on the left in each figure
d) shade the four tiles on the left in each figure
e) shade the central tile in each figure
f) shade the three tiles to the right in each figure

2. a)

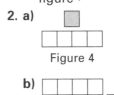

Figure 4

b)

Figure 4

c)

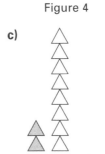

Figure 4

d)

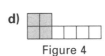

Figure 4

e)

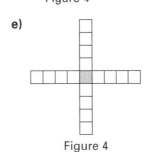

Figure 4

f)

Figure 4

3. a) $n + 1$ **b)** $2n + 1$ **c)** $2n + 2$ **d)** $n + 4$
   e) $4n + 1$ **f)** $3n + 3$
4. a) $3n + 2$, or $n + n + n + 2$; there are 11 tiles in Figure 3.
   b) $n + 4$; there are 7 tiles in Figure 3.
   c) $2n + 4$, or $n + n + 4$, or $2(n + 2)$; there are 10 toothpicks in Figure 3.
   d) $4n + 2$, or $2(2n + 1)$, or $n + n + n + n + 2$; there are 14 tiles in Figure 3.
5. $3n + 1$

Figure 1   Figure 2   Figure 3

4.3 The General Term of a Sequence

1. a) 13 **b)** 21 **c)** 37 **d)** 105
2. a)

Figure 4   Figure 5

   b) The missing values are 4, 5, 6, 7, and 8.
   c) $n + 3$
   d) 53
3. a) $2n + 1$
   b) 11 blocks; 21 blocks; 51 blocks; and 201 blocks
4. a) $2n + 5$ **b)** 19 tiles **c)** 39 tiles **d)** 145 tiles
5. a) $n + 7$; 19 and 37
   b) $2n + 2$; 26 and 62
   c) $3n + 6$; 42 and 96
   d) $5n + 1$; 61 and 151

4.4 Solve Problems by Examining Simpler Problems

1. a) 15 nickels and 7 dimes
   b) 380 cards
   c) 98 304 cans

4.5 Relating Number Sequences to Graphs

1. $4n + 3$
2. b) Pattern A: $4n$; Pattern B: $2n + 4$
   c) 28 and 18
   d) 5 and 8

Test Yourself

1. a) the unshaded part **b)** $3n + 2$
2. a) the bottom row of five tiles is shaded; $n + 5$
   b) the top two tiles are shaded; $2n + 2$
   c) no tiles are shaded; $3n$
   d) the two tiles to the right are shaded; $4n + 2$
3. a) $6n + 1$ **b)** $2n + 9$
4. a) 35 **b)** 82 **c)** 65
5. a) 7 **b)** 24 **c)** 4
6. a) The missing values are 18, 20, 22, 24, and 26.
   b) $2n + 10$ **c)** 110 **d)** 11
7. a) $n + 12$; 42 **b)** $2n + 8$; 68
8. 32 768
9. b) $3n + 6$ **c)** 18 **d)** 24

Chapter 5

5.1 Exploring Circles

1. a) A: radius, B: circumference
   b) C: diameter, D: chord, E: arc, F: semicircle
2. a) chords and arcs
   b) diameters and circumferences (or arcs)
3. a) Your design should use only curved lines.
   b) Your design should use only straight lines from one point on the circumference to another point on the circumference.

5.2 Exploring Circumference and Diameter

1. a) radius: 1.6 cm, diameter: 3.2 cm, circumference: 10.0 cm, $C \div r \doteq 6.3$, $C \div d \doteq 3.1$
   b) radius: 2.9 cm, diameter: 5.8 cm, circumference: 18.2 cm, $C \div r \doteq 6.3$, $C \div d \doteq 3.1$
2. $C \div r$ always equals about 6, and $C \div d$ always equals about 3.

5.3 Calculating Circumference

1. a) 12.6 cm **b)** 18.8 cm **c)** 25.1 cm **d)** 31.4 cm
   e) 14.4 cm **f)** 105.8 cm **g)** 226.4 cm
   h) 0.009 cm
2. a) 12.6 cm **b)** 31.4 cm **c)** 125.6 cm **d)** 2.51 cm
   e) 57.8 cm **f)** 79.8 cm **g)** 1284.9 cm
   h) 121.58 cm
3. a) 7 cm **b)** 19 m **c)** 32.5 mm **d)** 11.7 cm
   e) 56.3 m **f)** 44.25 cm
4. a) 7 cm **b)** 30 cm **c)** 0.2 cm **d)** 14.9 m
   e) 62.2 mm **f)** 16.1 cm

5. **a)** 7.5 cm **b)** 3.4 cm, 21.4 cm **c)** 7.4 m, 14.8 m
   d) 43.0 mm, 135.0 mm **e)** 4.95 cm, 9.90 cm
6. 79 cm
7. **a)** 239 m **b)** 136.6 m
8. **a)** estimate: about 180 cm; calculation:
   201 cm
   b) estimate: about 78 cm; calculation:
   79.8 cm
9. about 452 turns
10. **a)** 7.9 m **b)** $53.64

5.4 Estimating Area

1.

Dia-meter d	Circum-ference C	Radius r	Area A	(Radius)^2 r^2	$A \div r^2$
6 cm	18.84 cm	3 cm	28.26 cm^2	9 cm^2	3.14
12 cm	37.68 cm	6 cm	113.04 cm^2	36 cm^2	3.14
18 cm	56.52 cm	9 cm	254.34 cm^2	81 cm^2	3.14
24 cm	75.36 cm	12 cm	452.16 cm^2	144 cm^2	3.14
30 cm	94.2 cm	15 cm	706.5 cm^2	225 cm^2	3.14
36 cm	113.04 cm	18 cm	1017.36 cm^2	324 cm^2	3.14
42 cm	131.88 cm	21 cm	1384.74 cm^2	441 cm^2	3.14
48 cm	150.72 cm	24 cm	1808.64 cm^2	576 cm^2	3.14
54 cm	169.56 cm	27 cm	2289.06 cm^2	729 cm^2	3.14
60 cm	188.4 cm	30 cm	2826 cm^2	900 cm^2	3.14

2. 12.5 m^2
3. $141.30

5.5 Calculating Area

1. **a)** estimation: 300 cm^2; calculation: 314 cm^2
   b) estimation: 12 cm^2, calculation: 13 cm^2
   c) estimation: 108 cm^2, calculation: 113 cm^2
   d) estimation: 48 cm^2, calculation: 55.4 cm^2
   e) estimation: 30 000 cm^2,
   calculation: 32 476.7 cm^2
   f) estimation: 432 cm^2 calculation: 463.5 cm^2
2. 5.3 m^2
3. 660.2 km^2
4. **a)** 15.2 m^2 **b)** 28 cm^2

5.6 Solve Problems by Working Backward

1. **a)** 3.4 cm **b)** 9.1 m **c)** 5.5 cm
2. Your circle should have a radius of 1.7 cm.
3. **a)** 6 m^2 **b)** $744
4. 3.4 m

Test Yourself

1. **a)** radius **b)** chord
2. **a)** 38 cm **b)** 6 cm **c)** 1.6 cm **d)** 21.4 cm
   e) 36.7 cm **f)** 57.8 cm **g)** 393.29 cm
   h) 0.100 cm

3. **a)** 44 cm **b)** 82 cm **c)** 9.4 cm **d)** 20.7 cm
   e) 103.0 cm **f)** 558.35 cm
4. 51.5 cm
5. 13.0 m
6. 201.0 m
7. **a)** 28 cm^2 **b)** 907 cm^2 **c)** 0.5 cm^2
   d) 0.001 cm^2 **e)** 9.1 cm^2 **f)** 606.7 cm^2
   g) 3540.72 cm^2 **h)** 0.00005 cm^2
8. **a)** 50 cm^2 **b)** 615 cm^2 **c)** 179.0 cm^2
   d) 0.02 cm^2 **e)** 1.04 cm^2 **f)** 64.15 cm^2
   g) 785 000 cm^2 **h)** 0.00001 cm^2
9. 1.3 m^2
10. 66.4 m^2
11. **a)** 6 m **b)** 40 cm
12. **a)** 113 cm^2 **b)** 39 m^2 **c)** 298 cm^2 **d)** 107.5 m^2
    e) 9.4 cm^2 **f)** 52.6 cm^2

Chapter 6

6.1 Exploring Integer Addition and Subtraction

1. **a)** < **b)** > **c)** < **d)** > **e)** < **f)** <
2. **b)** 0 + 4 = 4
   c) 5 + (−8) = (−3)
3. **a)** 33 − 18 = 15
   b) 3 − (−23) = 26

6.2 Relating Integer Subtraction to Addition

1. **a)** No **b)** Yes **c)** Annika
2. **a)** 7 + 2 = 9
   b) (−3) + (−5) = (−8)
   c) 0 + (−5) = (−5)
   d) 1 + (−3) = (−2)
   e) 10 + 11 = 21
   f) (−4) + (−3) = (−7)
   g) (−2) + 4 = 2
   h) 7 + (−10) = (−3)
3. **a)** −9 **b)** −4 **c)** 10 **d)** 11 **e)** −9 **f)** −5 **g)** 1 **h)** 0
   i) −8 **j)** 2 **k)** 30 **l)** −8

6.3 Exploring Integer Multiplication

1. **a)** The missing values are 6, 0, and −9.
   b) 36, 24, 33
   c) −30, −60, −20
2. **a)** The missing values are −4 and 8.
   b) −12, −12, −42
   c) 25, 18, 24
3. **a)** positive integer
   b) negative integer
   c) positive integer
   d) negative integer

6.4 Multiplying Integers

1. Next, Teo subtracts. He crosses out eight black counters on the left side of the minus sign, and eight black counters on the right side. Eight positive (white) counters are left. The answer is 8.
2. **a)** -15 **b)** 6 **c)** 14 **d)** -10
3. Next, Tamara counts the number of units for the second set of arrows. The solid arrows go to the right 9 units. So the answer must be 9, which is the opposite of -9.
4. **a)** -5 **b)** 16 **c)** -21 **d)** 24
5. **a)** 72 **b)** 64 **c)** -8 **d)** 70 **e)** 75 **f)** -60 **g)** 160
   h) -68
6. **a)** $-5°C/min \times 13$ min $= -65°C$
   b) $8°C/day \times 3$ days $= 24°C$

6.5 Exploring Integer Division

1. Teo should divide the 10 counters into groups of 5. There will be 2 counters, each worth -1, in each group. So the answer is -2.
2. Selena should draw seven smaller, equally spaced arrows from -14 to 0. Each arrow covers two spaces below 0, so the answer is -2.
3. **a)** The missing values are 5 and -1.
   b) 7, 3, 9
   c) $-5, -7, -3$
4. **a)** The missing values are $-3, -1, 2$.
   b) $-8, -10, -4$
   c) 7, 16, 5
5. **a)** The pattern is: $-3, -2, -1, 1, 2, 3$
   b) The pattern is: 5, 3, 1, $-1, -3, -5$
6. **a)** positive integer
   b) negative integer
   c) positive integer
   d) negative integer

6.6 Dividing Integers

1. **b)** $(-6) \div (-2) = 3$
   c) $35 \div 7 = 5$
   d) $(-55) \div (-5) = 11$
   e) $8 \div (-8) = (-1)$
   f) $0 \div (-4) = 0$
2. **a)** $7 \times (-8) = (-56); (-8)$
   b) $3 \times (-10) = (-30); (-10)$
   c) $(-6) \times (-9) = 54; (-9)$
   d) $(-2) \times 11 = (-22) ; 11$
3. **a)** 13 **b)** -17 **c)** -4 **d)** 50 **e)** -3 **f)** -4
4. **a)** -2 **b)** -3 **c)** 8
5. **a)** -69 **b)** 8 **c)** -23 **d)** -32 **e)** -17 **f)** 22

6.7 Order of Operations with Integers

1. **a)** -36
   b) -1; The answers are different because the divisions are done in a different order in each question.
2. **a)** -8 **b)** -3 **c)** 4 **d)** 4 **e)** -6 **f)** -2
3. **a)** 6 **b)** -11 **c)** 22 **d)** 18 **e)** 5 **f)** -14
4. **a)** Nathan worked from left to right, but he subtracted before finishing all the multiplication.
   b) Selena started with subtraction instead of multiplication.
   c) 4
5. **a)** -6 **b)** -14 **c)** 1 **d)** -25 **e)** 21 **f)** 12
6. **a)** $[(-8) - 12] \div (-4) = 5$
   b) $[5 - (-5)] \times [(-4) + 2] = (-20)$
7. **a)** 4 **b)** -4 **c)** -7 **d)** -1
8. -233 m

6.8 Communicating about Calculations

1. Write an integer addition statement to show Teo's bank balance: $560 + (-55) + (-123) + 264 + (-45) = 601$. Teo has $601 in his bank account.
2. Start by writing an integer addition statement. Leave a blank for the original temperature: _____ $+ (-10°C) + 4°C = (-2)°C$. To find the answer, work backward starting from today. Remember to reverse the signs of the integers that represent changes in temperature: $(-2)°C + 10°C + (-4°C) = 4°C$. Two days ago, the temperature was $4°C$.
3. Assume the centre of the mall is 0 position, west is negative, and east is positive. Use an integer addition statement to describe Jordan's shopping: $(-25) + 16 + (-38) + 19 = (-28)$. Jordan is at position -28.

Test Yourself

1. **b)** $(-2) + (-1) = (-3)$
   c) $9 + (-7) = 2$
   d) $11 + (-20) = (-9)$
   e) $(-4) + 2 = (-2)$
   f) $7 + 3 = 10$
2. **a)** 5 **b)** -7 **c)** -14 **d)** -22 **e)** 12 **f)** 2 **g)** -2 **h)** 3
3. **a)** $5 \times (-3) = (-15)$
   b) $2 \times (-7) = (-14)$
   c) $(-3) \times (-4) = 12$
4. -18

●●●   ●●●   ●●●
●●●   ●●●   ●●●

5. a) 3 h $\times$ (−6 km/h) = (−18 km)
  b) 2 d $\times$ 5°C/d = 10°C
6. a) (−2) $\times$ ___ = 8
  b) (−1) $\times$ ___ = (−5)
  c) 2 $\times$ ___ = (−10)
  d) (−6) $\times$ ___ = 18
7. a) −30 **b)** −32 **c)** −2 **d)** −8 **e)** 25 **f)** −18 **g)** 4
  h) −70 **i)** −5 **j)** −55 **k)** 120 **l)** −60 **m)** 12 **n)** 2
  o) −2
8. a) −7956 **b)** 9968 **c)** −46 **d)** 61
9. a) −20 **b)** 0 **c)** 0 **d)** 2 **e)** 2 **f)** 23 **g)** 3 **h)** −6
10. a) 60 **b)** −12 **c)** 4 **d)** −1
11. 10°C + 3 $\times$ (−2°C) + 9°C = 13°C

Chapter 7

7.1 Coordinates of Points on a Grid

1. A: (2, 3), B: (5, −1), C: (−3, 4), D: (0, 2),
  E: (−1, −2), and F: (−4, 0)
2.

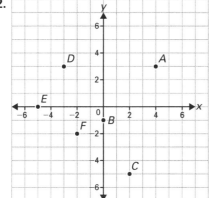

3. a) right **b)** left **c)** right **d)** right
4. a) above **b)** above **c)** below **d)** below
5. (6, 3)

7.2 Translations on a Coordinate System

1. a) (4, 6) **b)** (−3, 2) **c)** (11, 3) **d)** (−7, −13)
2. a)

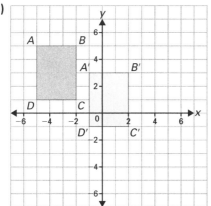

  b) A′(−1, 3), B′(2, 3), C′(2, −1), D′(−1, −1)

3. [−3, 1]
4. [5, −3]

7.3 Rotations and Reflections

1. a) (4, −5) **b)** (−3, −2) **c)** (−5, 7) **d)** (1, 5)
2. a) (−2, 2) **b)** (4, 1) **c)** (8, −3) **d)** (−4, −6)
3.

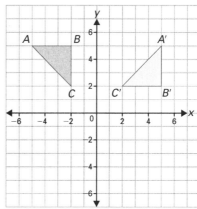

4.

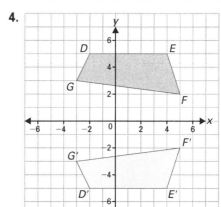

7.4 Exploring Similar Figures

1. b) Triangle *ABC* and triangle *DEF*: in lowest
    terms, all ratios are 1:2
    Triangle *GHI* and triangle *JLK*: in lowest
    terms, all ratios are 2:3
    Triangle *PQR* and triangle *ZXY*: in lowest
    terms, all ratios are 5:8
    Triangle *MNO* and triangle *TSU*: in lowest
    terms, all ratios are 3:4
  c) When comparing similar triangles, the
    ratios of corresponding sides are
    equivalent to each other.
2. The missing measures are 7 cm and 10 cm.

7.5 Communicating about Transformations

1. a) For example, Draw the points A(2, 4),
    B(6, 4), C(6, 2), and D(2, 2). Join the points
    to form a rectangle. Reflect this rectangle
    in the x-axis and draw the image.
  b) For example, Draw the points E(−3, −2),
    F(−1, −2), G(−1, −4), and H(−3, −4).

Join the points to form a square. Rotate this square 90°CW around the origin, and draw the image. Label the points of the image E', F', G', and H'. Rotate the second square a further 90°CW around the origin, and draw the new image. Label this image E", F", G", and H".

c) For example, "Draw the points J(−2, 2), K(0, 4), and L(2, 2). Join the points to form a triangle. Reflect the triangle in the x-axis, and draw the image. Label the points of the image J', K', and L'. Translate the image [4, 2], and draw the second image. Label the points of the second image J", K", and L"."

Test Yourself

1.
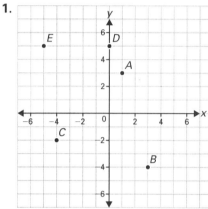

2. F, B, D, C, A, E
3. B, C, D, A, F, E
4. a) (4, 5) b) (3, −1) c) (4, 4) d) (−3, 2) e) (3, 1)
   f) (7, 8)
5. A'(0, 6), B'(2, 3), and C'(−2, 4)
6. E(−4, −3), F(−3, 1), G(−1, −2), and H(1, 3)
7. a)
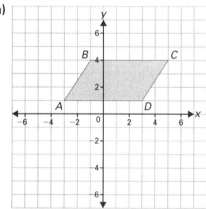

b) parallelogram
c) A'(−3, −1), B'(−1, −4), C'(5, −4), D'(3, −1)
d) A"(3, 1), B"(1, 4), C"(−5, 4), D"(−3, 1)
e) A'''(3, −1), B'''(1, −4), C'''(−5, −4), D'''(−3, −1)

8. a)
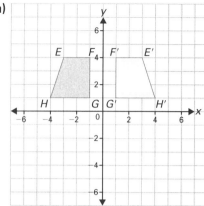

b)
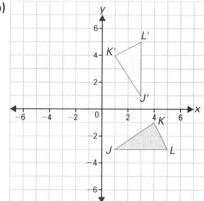

c)
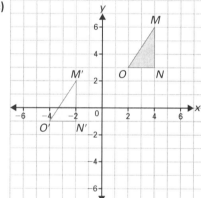

9. The missing measures are 9 cm and 2 cm.
10. a) 30°, 70°, and 80° b) 10 cm
11. Translate the triangle by [1, −2]. Draw the image. Next, reflect both triangles in the y-axis, and draw the image. Now reflect both sets of triangles in the x-axis, and draw the image.

Chapter 8

8.1 Solving Equations by Graphing

1. a) The missing values are 13, 19, and 25.
   b) The solution is 7.

Graph of 6n – 5

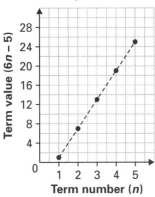

$6(7) - 5 = 42 - 5 = 37$

2. a)

Term number	1	2	3	4	5
Term value	6	8	10	12	14

b) $2n + 4$

c) $2n + 4 = 24$

d) The solution is 10.

Graph of a Sequence

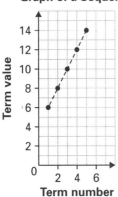

$2(10) + 4 = 20 + 4 = 24$

8.2 Representing Pattern Relationships

1. a)

Figure 1   Figure 2   Figure 3

b) The equation is $2n + 2$. To solve the equation, write $2n + 2 = 14$, so $2n = 12$, and $n = 6$. Rowyn made 14 trays of candy on the sixth day.

c) 8 days

8.3 Creating and Evaluating Algebraic Expressions

1. a) $20l + 30b$ **b)** $350

2. a) $1.25p + 0.75c$ **b)** $19

3. a) 13 **b)** 15 **c)** 9 **d)** 18 **e)** 30 **f)** 19

8.4 Solving Equations I

1. a) about 5 **b)** about 2 **c)** about 10 **d)** about 3

3. a) 4 **b)** 4 **c)** 8 **d)** 7 **e)** 2.5 **f)** 1.3 **g)** 2.2 **h)** 4.2

3. a) 4 **b)** 6.5 **c)** 7

4. 14.5

5. a) $20x = 200$, $x = 10$
   b) $7 - 3t = 1$, $t = 2$

6. b) about 7 or 8 times **c)** $78 + 15c = 198$
   d) 8 times

8.5 Solving Equations II

1. a) You need to subtract 2 counters from the right side.
   b) $3n + 2 = 8$ **c)** $n = 2$

2. a)

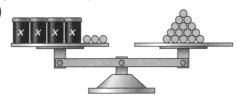

b) Subtract 3 marbles from each side.

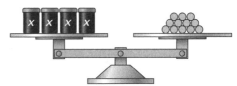

Divide both sides by 4.

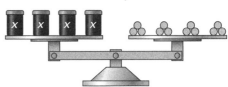

$x = 3$

3. a) 7 **b)** 3 **c)** 12 **d)** 3 **e)** 8 **f)** 7

4. a) $3b - 4 = 14$ **b)** six jewels

5. five marbles

6. a) 0.6 **b)** 7 **c)** 0.26

8.6 Communicating about Equations

1. a) The number of granola bars in each bag is represented by k. Rowyn bought three bags, so that represents $3k$. Rowyn's little brother eating 2 granola bars is the same as subtracting 2. The total number of granola bars at the end is 10.

b) $k = 4$

2. a) For example, "Paul bought four burgers. He also bought a drink costing $1.75. The total (not including tax) was $10.55. How much did each burger cost?"

b) $2.20

c) For example, "I chose b to represent the cost of one burger. Paul bought four burgers, so that was represented by $4b$. I needed to add 1.75, so I had Paul buy a drink for that amount. This represented $4b + 1.75$. Then I needed the total to be equal to 10.55, so I made this the cost of the meal."

Test Yourself

1. $x = 5$
2. **a)** $0.80x + 1.25y$ **b)** $5.70
3. **a)** The missing values are 16, 18 **b)** $2n + 8$
   c) $2n + 8 = 22$ **d)** $n = 7$
4. **a)** 30 **b)** 3 **c)** 50 **d)** 22.4
5. **a)** $2j + 3$ **b)** 27
6. **a)** $75f + 14c$ **b)** 351 g
7. **a)** 5 **b)** 7 **c)** 10 **d)** 6
8. 3 quarters
9. **a)** about 5 **b)** about 10 **c)** about 2 **d)** about 3
10. $b + 7 = 23$, $b = 16$
11. **a)**

   b) six marbles
12. For example: "Ping bought three pizzas. He also bought a drink for $1.70. His total (not including tax) came to $18.20. How much did each pizza cost?" The answer is $5.50.

Chapter 9

9.1 Adding and Subtracting Fractions Less Than 1

1. $\frac{9}{20}$
2. $\frac{1}{6}$
3. $\frac{22}{24}$, or $\frac{11}{12}$
4. **a)** $\frac{3}{8}$ **b)** $\frac{8}{15}$ **c)** $\frac{12}{32}$, or $\frac{3}{8}$
5. **a)** $\frac{9}{10} = \frac{18}{20}$ and $\frac{3}{4} = \frac{15}{20}$ **b)** $\frac{3}{20}$
6. **a)** $\frac{10}{24}$, or $\frac{5}{12}$ **b)** $\frac{7}{40}$ **c)** $\frac{8}{21}$

9.2 Adding and Subtracting Fractions Greater Than 1

1. **a)** $5\frac{4}{5}$ **b)** $4\frac{3}{4}$ **c)** $2\frac{3}{8}$ **d)** $5\frac{5}{10}$, or $5\frac{1}{2}$
2. **a)** 4 **b)** $4\frac{4}{5}$ **c)** $5\frac{1}{2}$ **d)** $8\frac{3}{4}$ **e)** $2\frac{7}{8}$ **f)** $8\frac{7}{10}$

3. **a)** $1\frac{2}{5}$ **b)** $1\frac{1}{4}$ **c)** $1\frac{2}{3}$ **d)** $2\frac{1}{5}$ **e)** $2\frac{3}{5}$ **f)** $\frac{1}{4}$
4. $3\frac{7}{8}$ cups
5. $4\frac{3}{40}$ tubes
6. $3\frac{1}{4}$ h
7. $6\frac{3}{4}$ min
8. $1\frac{7}{12}$ bags
9. **a)** $5\frac{7}{12}$ **b)** $\frac{1}{8}$ **c)** $4\frac{8}{9}$ **d)** $3\frac{11}{12}$ **e)** $6\frac{9}{14}$
   f) $\frac{3}{10}$ **g)** $2\frac{7}{15}$ **h)** $2\frac{23}{36}$ **i)** $3\frac{1}{4}$

9.3 Exploring Fraction Patterns

1. **a)** The missing fractions in the top row are $\frac{1}{64}$, $\frac{1}{128}$, and $\frac{1}{256}$. In the bottom row, they are $\frac{1}{32}$, $\frac{1}{64}$, and $\frac{1}{128}$.
   b) In the top row, the numerator is always 1. The denominator starts at 2 and is doubled in each subsequent term. In the bottom row, the numerator is always 1. The denominator starts at 4 and is doubled in each subsequent term.
2. **a)** The missing fractions in the top row are $\frac{1}{1024}$, $\frac{1}{4096}$, and $\frac{1}{16384}$. In the bottom row, they are $\frac{5}{1024}$, $\frac{5}{4096}$, $\frac{5}{16384}$.
   b) In the top row, the numerator is always 1. The denominator starts at 4 and is multiplied by 4 to get each subsequent term. You could also say that the denominator is 4^n. In the bottom row, the numerator is always 5. The denominator starts at 16 and is multiplied by 4 to get each subsequent term. You could also say that the denominator is $4^n \times 4$.
   c) The 10th term in the top row will be $\frac{1}{4^{10}}$, or $\frac{1}{1\,048\,576}$. The 10th term in the bottom row will be $\frac{5}{(4^{10} \times 4)}$, or $\frac{5}{4\,194\,304}$.
   d) For the top row, the algebraic expression is $\frac{1}{4^n}$. For the bottom row, the algebraic expression is $\frac{5}{(4^n \times 4)}$.

9.4 Fractions of Fractions

1. For example:

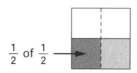

$\frac{1}{2}$ of $\frac{1}{2}$ —→

2. **a)** The circle is divided into two parts, and one part is shaded. This shows $\frac{1}{2}$. Each part is further divided into quarters, and one of these quarters is shaded. This shows $\frac{1}{4}$ of $\frac{1}{2}$. Since there are 8 parts in total, and 1 part is shaded, this shows that $\frac{1}{4}$ of $\frac{1}{2}$ is $\frac{1}{8}$.

   b) The shape is divided into quarters, and one part is shaded. This shows $\frac{1}{4}$. Each part is further divided into thirds, and one part is shaded. This shows $\frac{1}{3}$ of $\frac{1}{4}$. Since there are 12 parts in total, and 1 part is shaded, this shows that $\frac{1}{3}$ of $\frac{1}{4}$ is $\frac{1}{12}$.

3. For example:

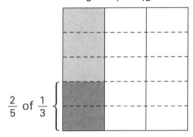

$\frac{2}{5}$ of $\frac{1}{3}$

4. **a)** 1 **b)** 2 or 1 **c)** 24 or 8 **d)** 2 or 1

9.5 Multiplying Fractions

1. **a)** When using direct multiplication, Hoshi did not need to multiply the numerator of $\frac{2}{5}$ by both 3 and 4, and the denominator by both 3 and 4. Instead, he should have multiplied the numerator of $\frac{2}{5}$ by 3 (the numerator of $\frac{3}{4}$), and the denominator of $\frac{2}{5}$ by 4 (the denominator of $\frac{3}{4}$).

   b) The correct answer is $\frac{3}{10}$.

2. **a)** $\frac{1}{3} \times \frac{1}{5}$ **b)** $\frac{5}{6} \times \frac{1}{2}$

3. **a)** $\frac{4}{20}$ or $\frac{1}{5}$ **b)** $\frac{1}{9}$ **c)** $\frac{8}{21}$

4. **a)** $\frac{6}{25}$ **b)** $\frac{12}{35}$ **c)** $\frac{15}{28}$ **d)** $\frac{15}{32}$ **e)** $\frac{5}{16}$ **f)** $\frac{21}{40}$ **g)** $\frac{6}{35}$

   h) $\frac{6}{40}$ or $\frac{3}{20}$ **i)** $\frac{21}{80}$

5. $\frac{3}{20}$

6. $\frac{14}{3}$, or $4\frac{2}{3}$ cans

7. $\frac{21}{32}$ of the package

9.6 Multiplying Fractions Greater Than 1

1. **a)** about $\frac{2}{3}$ **b)** a little less than $5\frac{1}{2}$

   c) a little less than 12 **d)** a little more than 4

2. **a)** $5\frac{1}{5}$ **b)** $8\frac{5}{8}$

3. **a)** $1\frac{1}{8}$ **b)** $4\frac{2}{3}$ **c)** $7\frac{1}{3}$ **d)** $9\frac{5}{8}$ **e)** $10\frac{2}{3}$ **f)** 372

4. 12.5 min

9.7 Dividing Fractions I

1. **a)** 2 **b)** 3 **c)** 4 **d)** $\frac{2}{3}$ **e)** 6 **f)** $\frac{3}{10}$

2.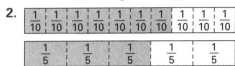

3. **a)** $\frac{9}{2}$, or $4\frac{1}{2}$ **b)** $\frac{2}{5}$ **c)** $\frac{21}{16}$ or $1\frac{5}{16}$ **d)** $\frac{3}{5}$ **e)** $\frac{10}{27}$

   f) $\frac{20}{21}$

4. **a)** $\frac{10}{3}$ or $3\frac{1}{3}$ **b)** $\frac{9}{10}$ **c)** $\frac{81}{40}$, or $2\frac{1}{40}$

5. 15 rows

9.8 Dividing Fractions II

1. **a)** $\frac{5}{2}$ **b)** $\frac{4}{3}$ **c)** $\frac{2}{1}$, or 2 **d)** $\frac{6}{5}$ **e)** $\frac{10}{3}$ **f)** $\frac{3}{2}$ **g)** $\frac{8}{5}$

   h) $\frac{5}{4}$ **i)** $\frac{1}{5}$

2. **a)** $\frac{3}{5}$ **b)** $\frac{10}{13}$ **c)** $\frac{4}{9}$ **d)** $\frac{4}{11}$ **e)** $\frac{6}{23}$ **f)** $\frac{10}{19}$ **g)** $\frac{3}{7}$ **h)** $\frac{8}{21}$

   i) $\frac{6}{25}$

3. **a)** 1 **b)** 1 **c)** 1 **d)** 1

4. **a)** $4 \times \frac{2}{1} = 8$ **b)** $\frac{4}{5} \times \frac{1}{2} = \frac{2}{5}$ **c)** $\frac{1}{2} \times \frac{4}{3} = \frac{2}{3}$

   d) $\frac{5}{6} \times \frac{3}{2} = \frac{5}{4}$

5. **a)** $\frac{3}{10}$ **b)** $1\frac{1}{20}$ **c)** $1\frac{7}{18}$ **d)** $\frac{3}{8}$ **e)** $1\frac{1}{2}$ **f)** $2\frac{1}{2}$ **g)** $\frac{1}{8}$

   h) $\frac{1}{5}$ **i)** $1\frac{1}{4}$ **j)** $2\frac{6}{7}$ **k)** $\frac{1}{16}$ **l)** 25

6. **a)** $\frac{21}{8}$ or $2\frac{5}{8}$ **b)** $\frac{65}{3}$ or $21\frac{2}{3}$ **c)** $\frac{23}{9}$ or $2\frac{5}{9}$

7. 28 glasses

8. $1\frac{5}{9}$ walls

9.9 Communicating about Multiplication and Division

1. **a)** $\frac{3}{4}$ **b)** $\frac{2}{5}$ **c)** $\frac{5}{8}$ **d)** $\frac{1}{2}$

2. First, convert $0.4 \div 0.2$ into fractions to get $\frac{4}{10} \div \frac{2}{10}$. You want to find out how many 2 tenths fit into 4 tenths. $4 \div 2$ means how many sets of 2 of anything are in 4 of that thing. So $4 \div 2$ has the same answer as $0.4 \div 0.2$.

3. First, convert 0.5 into a fraction, to get $\frac{5}{10}$ or $\frac{1}{2}$. This means that you need $\frac{1}{2}$ of a set of 2.6. Next, convert 2.6 into a fraction, to get $\frac{26}{10}$ or $2\frac{6}{10}$. Don't bother to simplify into lowest terms, since it will be easier to find $\frac{1}{2}$ of this fraction. Draw a picture to show $2\frac{6}{10}$. For example,

Use a different colour to shade $\frac{1}{2}$ of the shaded squares. 1 and $\frac{3}{10}$ of the rectangles are shaded with this colour. In decimal form, this is equal to 1.3. So $0.5 \times 2.6 = 1.3$.

4. First, find the reciprocal of the second fraction. The reciprocal of $\frac{1}{8}$ is $\frac{8}{1}$. Next, use the reciprocal to write the equivalent multiplication. $\frac{1}{4} \div \frac{1}{8}$ is the same as $\frac{1}{4} \times \frac{8}{1}$. To multiply the fractions, multiply the numerators and the denominators. $\frac{1}{4} \times \frac{8}{1} = \frac{1 \times 8}{4 \times 1} = \frac{8}{4} = 2$. The answer is 2.

9.10 Order of Operations

1. a) $\frac{3}{4}$ **b)** 1 **c)** $\frac{25}{30}$ **d)** $\frac{3}{4}$ **e)** $1\frac{3}{10}$ **f)** $\frac{2}{5}$

2. a) < **b)** < **c)** > **d)** >

3. a) $\frac{11}{12}$ **b)** 3 **c)** $1\frac{5}{19}$ **d)** $4\frac{5}{12}$

Test Yourself

1. a) $\frac{3}{4}$ **b)** $1\frac{1}{8}$ **c)** $\frac{1}{10}$ **d)** $\frac{3}{4}$

2. a) $\frac{1}{2}$ **b)** $\frac{5}{8}$ **c)** $\frac{17}{18}$ **d)** $\frac{1}{20}$ **e)** $1\frac{4}{21}$ **f)** $\frac{2}{15}$ **g)** $\frac{11}{12}$

   h) $3\frac{1}{5}$

3. Sheree ate more.

4. a) $1\frac{5}{8}$ **b)** $3\frac{8}{15}$

5. a) 6 **b)** $3\frac{1}{4}$ **c)** $3\frac{5}{6}$ **d)** $1\frac{1}{8}$ **e)** $3\frac{23}{30}$ **f)** $5\frac{11}{20}$

6. $5\frac{7}{10}$ packages of cookies

7. For example:

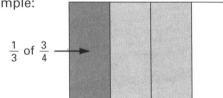

$\frac{1}{3}$ of $\frac{3}{4}$ →

8. a) $\frac{1}{10}$ **b)** $\frac{5}{8}$

9. a) $\frac{1}{8}$ of the summer **b)** $\frac{5}{8}$ of the summer

10. a) $\frac{11}{30}$ **b)** $4\frac{2}{7}$ **c)** $4\frac{1}{16}$ **d)** $6\frac{2}{3}$ **e)** $8\frac{1}{3}$ **f)** $\frac{3}{50}$

11. a) 5 **b)** $\frac{1}{5}$

12. a) 18 **b)** $9\frac{1}{3}$ **c)** $\frac{1}{4}$ **d)** $\frac{2}{5}$ **e)** $1\frac{5}{16}$ **f)** $\frac{7}{8}$

13. $1\frac{13}{15}$ pages per minute

14. Teo is correct. $\frac{8}{9} \div \frac{1}{9}$ is the same as $\frac{8}{9} \div \frac{1}{3} \times \frac{1}{3}$. This is equal to the first expression times $\frac{1}{3}$.

15. a) 1 **b)** $\frac{1}{5}$ **c)** $\frac{121}{288}$ **d)** $2\frac{4}{7}$

Chapter 10

10.1 Exploring Points on a Circle

1. u and v, u and y, w and x

2.

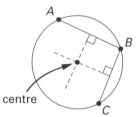

   d) This point is equidistant to points A, B, and C because it is the centre of the circle, and the three other points are on the rim of the circle.

3.

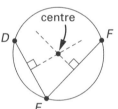

10.2 Intersecting Lines, Parallel Lines, and Transversals

1. a) 20° **b)** 65° **c)** 105° **d)** 50° **e)** 165° **f)** 15°

2. The missing angles are 150°, 30°, and 150°.

10.3 Angles in a Triangle

1. a) 70° **b)** 48° **c)** 105° **d)** 9°

2. a) 60° **b)** 21° **c)** 87° **d)** 42°

3. 45°

4. 100°

5. This triangle is not possible because the sum of the angles is greater than 180°.

10.4 Exploring Quadrilaterals

1. a) $\angle a = 35°$, $\angle b = 45°$, $\angle c = 100°$
   b) $\angle d = 60°$, $\angle e = 65°$, $\angle f = 60°$

c) $\angle g = 50°$, $\angle h = 45°$
d) $\angle m = 80°$
2. **a)** 65° **b)** 88° **c)** 145° **d)** 146°

10.5 Exploring Right Triangles

1. **a)** The areas are 9 square units, 16 square units, and 25 square units. 9 + 16 = 25
   b) The areas are 36 square units, 64 square units, and 100 square units. 36 + 64 = 100
   c) The areas are 25 square units, 144 square units, and 169 square units.
   25 + 144 = 169
2. For example, "When a square is drawn on each side of a right-angled triangle, the sum of the areas of the two smallest squares is equal to the area of the largest square."

10.6 Applying the Pythagorean Theorem

1. **a)** 7.2 **b)** 7.9 **c)** 6.9 **d)** 7.5 **e)** 7.6 **f)** 8.1
2. **a)** 75 cm² **b)** 5.3 cm²
3. **a)** 4.6 cm **b)** 16.3 cm **c)** 14.2 cm **d)** 3.2 cm
   e) 18.9 cm **f)** 2.7 cm
4. 17 cm
5. 20 km
6. 4.0 m
7. 29.75 m²

10.7 Solve Problems Using Logical Reasoning

1. isosceles
2. 18.6 m
3. **a)** 5.9 m **b)** 5.6 m

Test Yourself

1. For example: adjacent angles: *a* and *b*, opposite angles: *e* and *g*, corresponding angles: *g* and *c*, supplementary angles: *h* and *e* (or *h* and *a*)
2. **a)** 125° **b)** 96° **c)** 30° **d)** 108°
3. **a)** 35° **b)** 60° **c)** 75° **d)** 62°
4. $\angle a = 142°$, $\angle b = 38°$, $\angle c = 112°$, $\angle d = 30°$
5. **a)** 60° **b)** 45° **c)** 124° **d)** 37°
6. **a)** 130° **b)** 138° **c)** 44°
7. **a)** 7.2 cm **b)** 19.7 cm **c)** 30.5 cm **d)** 4.8 cm
8. 50°
9. 4.8 m
10. 24.8 m

Chapter 11

11.1 Exploring Cylinders

1. **a)** B, E, D, A, C **b)** E, C, A, D, B
2. 31.4 cm

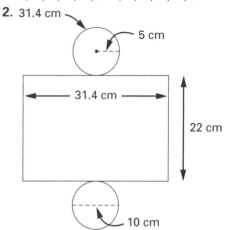

11.2 Surface Area of a Cylinder

1. 127 cm
2. **a)** about 85 square units
   b) about 236 square units
3. **a)** 18.84 cm² **b)** 414 cm² **c)** 1011 cm²
   d) 339 cm²
4. **a)** 339.1 cm² **b)** 16.6 cm² **c)** 28.3 cm²
   d) 410.9 cm²
5. **a)** 251.2 cm² **b)** 4.0 cm² **c)** 1623.6 cm²
   d) 127.4 cm²

11.3 The Volume of a Cylinder

1. **a)** about 162 cm³ **b)** about 30 cm³
   c) about 36 000 cm³
2. **a)** 550 cm³ **b)** 0.2 cm³ **c)** 107.9 cm³
   d) 7254.7 cm³
3. 17.0 cm

11.4 Solve Problems Using Diagrams

1. **a)** 141 cm³ **b)** 108 cm³
2. 850 cm²

11.5 Exploring the Platonic Solids

1. See the table at the bottom of the page.

11.6 Polyhedron Faces, Edges, and Vertices

1. 8 edges
2. 12 faces
3. **a)** 5 + 6 − 9 = 2 **b)** 8 + 12 − 18 = 2
   c) 6 + 6 − 10 = 2 **d)** 8 + 12 − 18 = 2
4. Tran is correct, because 11 + 5 − 14 = 2.

1. **a)** 824 cm² **b)** 16.7 cm² **c)** 301.4 cm² **d)** 39.9 cm²
2. 138 cm²
3. 2238.8 cm²
4. Cylinder A
5. 103.2 m³
6. **a)** 141 cm³ **b)** 1.2 cm³ **c)** 13 349.8 cm³
   d) 512.4 cm³
7. **a)** 30 521 cm³ **b)** 182.1 cm³
8. 936 cm³
9. $6 + 8 - 12 = 2$

Chapter 12

12.1 Exploring Theoretical and Experimental Probability

1. **a)** $\frac{1}{2}$, or 1 out of 2 **b)** 0 **c)** $\frac{1}{4}$, or 1 out of 4

2. $\frac{1}{8}$, or 1 out of 8

3. 60%

4. **a)** $\frac{1}{6}$, or 1 out of 6 **b)** $\frac{3}{6}$, or 1 out of 2

   c) $\frac{3}{6}$, or 1 out of 2 **d)** 0

5. **a)** $\frac{5}{9}$, or 5 out of 9 **b)** $\frac{4}{9}$, or 4 out of 9

6. No. A probability of 1 means 100% certainty.
   This is the greatest possible probability.

12.2 Theoretical and Experimental Probabilities

1. **a)** $\frac{1}{2}$ **b)** $\frac{1}{8}$ **c)** $\frac{3}{8}$

2. **a)** $\frac{1}{2}$ **b)** $\frac{1}{4}$ **c)** $\frac{1}{4}$

3. Manuel's experimental probability was
   close but not the same as the theoretical
   probability in question 1. The experimental
   probability of getting a green marble
   was the same as the theoretical probability.

The experimental probability of getting a red marble was a little greater than the theoretical probability, and the experimental probability of getting a white marble was a little less.

12.3 Calculating Probabilities

1. **a)**

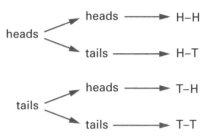

b) four **c)** $\frac{1}{4}$ **d)** $\frac{1}{2}$

2. **a)**

Coloured spinner	Numbered spinner	Outcome
white	1	(white, 1)
	2	(white, 2)
	3	(white, 3)
grey	1	(grey, 1)
	2	(grey, 2)
	3	(grey, 3)

b) assuming the spinners are spun at the
same time (in no particular order), there
are six possible outcomes

c) $\frac{1}{6}$

3. **a)**

(W,R)	(W,R)	(W,R)	(W,R)	(W,R)	(W,R)
(1, 1)	(2, 1)	(3, 1)	(4, 1)	(5, 1)	(6, 1)
(1, 2)	(2, 2)	(3, 2)	(4, 2)	(5, 2)	(6, 2)
(1, 3)	(2, 3)	(3, 3)	(4, 3)	(5, 3)	(6, 3)
(1, 4)	(2, 4)	(3, 4)	(4, 4)	(5, 4)	(6, 4)
(1, 5)	(2, 5)	(3, 5)	(4, 5)	(5, 5)	(6, 5)
(1, 6)	(2, 6)	(3, 6)	(4, 6)	(5, 6)	(6, 6)

b) 36 outcomes **c)** $\frac{1}{36}$ **d)** $\frac{4}{9}$ **e)** $\frac{1}{18}$

Polyhedron	Type of polygon	Number of faces (in total)	Number of vertices (in total)	Number of edges (in total)	Number of faces at each vertex
Tetrahedron	equilateral triangle	4	4	6	3
Octahedron	equilateral triangle	8	6	12	4
Icosahedron	equilateral triangle	20	12	30	5
Cube	square	6	8	12	3
Dodecahedron	regular pentagon	12	20	30	3